Haunted Bordentown

Arlene S. Bice

4880 Lower Valley Road, Atglen, Pennsylvania 19310

Dedication

To my dearest friends, especially Anne Peterson, Tom Moyer and Pete Hobday. Their presence in my life has made it better.

Schiffer Books are available at special discounts for bulk purchases for sales promotions or premiums. Special editions, including personalized covers, corporate imprints, and excerpts can be created in large quantities for special needs. For more information contact the publisher:

Published by Schiffer Publishing Ltd.
4880 Lower Valley Road
Atglen, PA 19310
Phone: (610) 593-1777; Fax: (610) 593-2002
E-mail: Info@schifferbooks.com

For the largest selection of fine reference books on this and related subjects, please visit our web site at **www.schifferbooks.com**
We are always looking for people to write books on new and related subjects. If you have an idea for a book please contact us at the above address.

This book may be purchased from the publisher.
Include $3.95 for shipping.
Please try your bookstore first.
You may write for a free catalog.

In Europe, Schiffer books are distributed by
Bushwood Books
6 Marksbury Ave.
Kew Gardens
Surrey TW9 4JF England
Phone: 44 (0) 20 8392-8585; Fax: 44 (0) 20 8392-9876
E-mail: info@bushwoodbooks.co.uk
Website: www.bushwoodbooks.co.uk
Free postage in the U.K., Europe; air mail at cost.

Other Schiffer Books on Related Subjects:
Ghosts of New York City, 0-7643-1714-8, $12.95
Ghosts of Valley Forge and Phoenixville, 978-0-76432633-2, $14.95
Schiffer Publishing has a wide variety of books about ghosts and the supernatural. Please visit our web site for more great titles.

Copyright © 2008 by Arlene S. Bice
Library of Congress Control Number: 2007941874

All rights reserved. No part of this work may be reproduced or used in any form or by any means—graphic, electronic, or mechanical, including photocopying or information storage and retrieval systems—without written permission from the publisher.
The scanning, uploading and distribution of this book or any part thereof via the Internet or via any other means without the permission of the publisher is illegal and punishable by law. Please purchase only authorized editions and do not participate in or encourage the electronic piracy of copyrighted materials.
"Schiffer," "Schiffer Publishing Ltd. & Design," and the "Design of pen and ink well" are registered trademarks of Schiffer Publishing Ltd.

Designed by Mark David Bowyer
Type set in A Charming Font Expanded / NewsGoth BT

ISBN: 978-0-7643-2859-6
Printed in China

Contents

Disclaimer 5

Acknowledgments 7

Introduction 9

Definitions 15

Part One: Town Happenings 17
   'Spirit Kids' Run Amuck 19
   Who's Living in Our House 24
   Fred, the Friendly Ghost 26
   The Spectral Family 31
   The Happy Child 34
   The Jolly Ghosts 37
   Blessing the Spirits 41
   The Maternal Ghost 46
   A Ghostly Warning.....................................56
   Generations of Psychic Ability 59
   The Ghostly Painter...................................68
   'The Lady' Who Never Left 71
   Anchored to His Home?.................................81
   Someone to Look Over Me 84
   The Eerie Basement................................... 88
   A Reassuring Presence 91

Ghosts Are Knocking 94
Unfriendly Housewarming 98
Inheriting the Rituals 100
The Mischievous Ghost 102

Part Two: Historical Haunts 107
The Clara Barton Schoolhouse 107
The Secret Room 115
Old Ironsides 118
The Idell Affair 123
Bellevue 127
Burr's Corner 133

Part Three: Township Sightings 135
More Than One Ghost 136
The Wounded Ghost? 141

Part Four: Area Hauntings 143
The Unsettled House in Cranbury 143
Ghostly Remnants in Hightstown 146

Part Five: Rumors 147
The Old Opera House 147
Waretown Mennonites 149
Lenni Lenape Indians 150
The Jersey Devil 152

Part Six: Afterthoughts 155

Bibliography 158

Index 159

Disclaimer

The stories published here with the written permission of the persons who have repeated their experiences to me or have been offered to the public through the Ghost Walk conducted in Bordentown City, originated by me. I am not a professional ghost hunter or claim any expertise with the Spirit World. I am a collector of stories and a writer with my own personal psychic experiences.

All rights reserved. No part of this publication may be reproduced or transmitted in any form or means without the written permission from the publisher.

Acknowledgments

I'm deeply grateful to many people who made this book possible. Firstly, many thanks go to my editor, Dinah Roseberry, for suggesting the book and sharing her enthusiasm of ghosts and spirits. She responded quickly to my every question with suggestions and guidelines, giving me honest answers to my many queries. It's so important to have a person with a good attitude to go to with a thought or problem.

Also thank you to Editor Jennifer Marie Savage for her good advice and guidance.

A big thank you goes to the many people who shared their stories and updated their earlier stories to keep us informed on the events in their lives so we can enjoy, learn, and understand the experiences of others. This book couldn't have come together without their trust and their stories. They gave me permission to share these stories with the public. Of this, I am grateful. Please respect their privacy.

I'm indebted to sister-writer, InSuk Granholm, who nagged me into joining the International Women's Writing Guild (IWWG) and then nagged me into going to my first IWWG conference at Skidmore. I haven't missed a year since that first one in 1999. Her nagging changed my life entirely, going from good to even better.

It's impossible to give enough thanks to Hannelore Hahn, founder of the International Women Writers' Guild, to Elizabeth Julia, who always cheerfully finds answers for my questions, to the workshop leaders at the Skidmore Annual Women Writers' Conferences and IWWG's members. They are the women who guided, prodded, and encouraged me to bring forth memories I thought were forgotten and sparked new ideas that I needed. To all of them I am deeply grateful.

A huge thank you goes to Betty Ann Burke, my trusted and very competent researcher who finds what I need and sends it to me when I need it. I would be lost without her help.

Finally, many thanks go to the wonderful people of historic Bordentown City, New Jersey. To all those who walked into my shop offering fascinating conversations, exchanges of ideas and thoughts. Bordentonians are caring, kind, interested, and interesting people. Once you've truly lived there, you are always bound to it and carry the heart of the town with you wherever you go.

Introduction

When my book, *Ghosts of Bordentown,* was published, many were surprised and excited, especially Bordentonians. A floodgate opened. Instead of water, stories of further hauntings came forth. Stories came in from Bordentown Township, too. This was unexpected because I thought of the township as being new. A foolish idea. The Lenape Indians were here long before the Quaker settlers came in the 1600s, and early pioneers also settled in the township, especially along the creeks and waterways.

Besides, hauntings, ghosts, and spirit visits don't always come from long ago, and it isn't necessary to be psychically developed to get a visit after a loved one dies. You only need to be open to the moment. We don't think of those happenings as ghosts, but just visits from a loved one who wants to be remembered by us.

In my research, I've read about and met people who are afraid of dying, of being dead, of being buried in the ground or burned up into ashes. Mediums and psychics say that you don't die. You shed your physical body as you would shed your clothes at night before going to bed. Your spirit remains. It doesn't die, but goes over to the next plane, which is not a removal to somewhere else but is just out of our sight. Or at least out of the sight of the average person.

Mostly I've used the terms "passed on" or "passed over" in the following stories to replace the old idea of the body dying being the end of life. It is only the end of life, as we know it. Our spirit goes on. Occasionally I've used the term "died" or "dead," although I think of those words differently since I've experienced moments from the afterlife.

Psychics, mediums and anyone with a developed sixth sense often see spirits, but don't tell people for fear of frightening the naïve. We each have psychic ability. Too many people refuse to develop this additional gift out of fear of the unknown and because they are afraid of ridicule.

I learned to face my fears and my deepest sorrows of loss years ago, to learn about what frightened me and why. The more I read from all avenues, the more I learned to understand, and the less fear I carried.

When my first-born son, Kenny, died in an automobile accident in 1982 at age twenty-four, I kept myself too busy to mourn. I built invisible walls that protected me from sorrow and probably kept me from being contacted by him... but I did begin to search for answers and understanding.

When my third-born son, Guy, died in a boating accident in 1988 at age twenty-five, I wept openly and often at my loss of having him near me. But my sorrow was different because I knew he fulfilled his life as he was supposed to do. His staying on earth couldn't have completed his life anymore. He attained what he was supposed to attain in this lifetime. So his life journey ended early.

I remember the first time he "came" to me. I was working in my gift shop and he fluffed my hair behind my right ear. I knew it was Guy and I knew he was just fine. He came to me rather often over the next seventeen years. More than once a psychic walked into my shop (I think the crystals hanging in my shop window attracted mediums and psychics) and we would wind up in a great conversation. One day a medium said to me, "Your son is standing behind you." Then, "Oh, I'm so sorry. I hope I didn't upset you. It just popped out!" I just smiled contentedly replying, "Thanks, but I always know when he's here with me."

A month before my mother *passed over* at seventy-two years old, she told me her mother came to her in dreams a couple nights in a row. "I can't remember the last time I even thought of my mother," she told me.

Then, during the last two weeks before her passing, she was visited several nights by her close friend of fifty years. Annie was calling her, beckoning her...and coming to make her transition less frightening. The afternoon of her passing, I stopped in after work as I did every day. Mom was sitting in her favorite chair asleep. At least I thought she was asleep until I saw that her false teeth had dropped. Then I knew she was gone from this earth. She was the picture of peace. I guess Annie made it easier for her.

Twenty years later I was visiting with Annie's daughter. She told me her mother came for her husband on three successive nights at the end of a lengthy illness. He adored his mother-in-law and spoke to her while his wife (my friend) sat in the corner of his hospital room. She didn't see a thing.

In furthering my research I read that scientists have conducted experiments to prove that a person's own electricity caused the sensation of seeing ghosts. But the very same experiments seemed to prove to the believers in the spiritual world that the scientists only proved what the spiritualists always believed to be true.

Madame Marie Curie, during her early research with radioactive elements, attended séances to observe the powers of mediums. British physicists J. J. Thompson, John Strutt, and Nobel Prize winner Lord Rayleigh did the same. Lord Rayleigh later joined in on researching the paranormal, as did other physicists including wireless radio pioneer Sir Oliver Lodge.

American psychologist and philosopher William James, brother to literary author Henry James, leaned heavily on the idea that scientists deadened the willingness of people to admit they had paranormal experiences. Ridicule is difficult to accept for most people. This is the same reason children lose their natural ability to communicate with spirits. Adults pooh-pooh their comments and say, "That's all imaginary, dear."

The stories from my first ghost book were developed for the Ghost Walk I conducted for my business group, the Downtown Bordentown Association, as a fundraiser when I ran a used bookshop there. It was an evening of entertainment and a door to open for further exploration into a subject I didn't fully understand at the time. I had seen ghosts and experienced other bizarre moments, but never had the avenue to explore and gain a deeper perception.

Since then people have come to know me as a woman to talk to about strange happenings. If they were exposed to paranormal phenomena and didn't feel comfortable talking about it to most people, they heard I would welcome their experiences without ridicule.

There are reasons for these instances. Some people are more open and receptive to psychic experiences. It's been said that we all have extrasensory perception, but some of us develop it more than others. My grandmother, Elizabeth Urbanski Daniels, was born with a veil on her face and paranormal abilities. The veil is a thin layer of skin that covers part or all of the face at birth. It's sometimes called a cowl. It indicates a fully developed psychic ability.

My mother, Anna May Bice Riggi, had extraordinary extra-sensory perception where her children were concerned. She knew I was pregnant before I did even though she was 1,200 miles away. She also telephoned within five minutes after my brother's car was demolished, living the same distance apart. She knew something dreadful had happened, but didn't know what it was.

I've had moments throughout my life when I was fully aware of my psychic abilities. Although I never paid much attention to them until after my first-born son passed over at twenty-four years old. That's when I began to search for answers about things I didn't understand.

This same son, Kenny, came racing into the house one hot summer afternoon when he was about six years old. "Mommy, Daddy's on fire!" I knew his father was in the bedroom sleeping. To reassure him that everything was okay, I took him by the hand to peek into the bedroom. To my surprise, the electric extension cord to the air conditioner was sparking flames! Surely my son saved his father's life.

Many times people are contacted by loved ones or others who have passed on, but those experiences aren't really considered ghostly. They are just visits. Too often folks just explain those happenings away rather than face the truth about what could be a wonderful moment. Sometimes there is a message and sometimes it is just to let you know that all is well.

In the following stories you'll read of hauntings, personal ghosts and house ghosts, astral travel and visits. It seems that remodeling or changing a house physically stirs up sleeping ghosts. That theme seems to run through many of the stories here. Some of the stories have local history behind them from different periods of time. Some ghosts are obviously still confused; some I think are just bound to a happy place and time. There are several stories with a child or children as the main subject.

To protect the privacy of our generous witnesses to the ghostly happenings of Bordentown, I've used only first names and general areas. The book was written for you to enjoy, and I hope you do so. Remember, if you decide to go ghost hunting, walk lightly and keep in mind that many ghosts are lost, kind, and gentle spirits.

Enjoy,
Arlene S. Bice

PS: While writing this introduction, the computer constantly doubled my consonants and broke contact between my mouse and the screen. This didn't happen while I was writing the stories...only when I delved into comparisons between scientists and psychical research.

Definitions

Telepathy — A person's awareness of another's thoughts without using any normal channels.

Clairvoyance — Knowledge acquired of an object or event without the use of the senses.

Precognition — Knowledge of another person's future, thoughts or events.

Psychokinesis — A person's ability to influence a physical object or an event merely by thinking about it.

Clairaudience — Psychic ability to hear voices and other auditory phenomena.

Clairaudient — Also called Supranormal Hearing, it's receiving messages from those who have *passed over*.

Planchette Board — A device ostensibly used for obtaining messages from the spirit world, often employed by a medium during a séance. Many use this as a game board. The concept goes back to 540 BC.

Veil — A fine layer of skin over half or all of the face at birth. It indicates a fully developed extrasensory perception. Also called a cowl.

Medium — One who communicates with entities in the spirit world.

ESP — Extra-sensory perception.

Synchronicity — Meaningful coincidental events.

Part One:

Town Happenings

Bordentown City is one square mile located in a pocket between the Delaware River, State Highway 206, and State Highway 130. These physical surroundings have created a safe area...like a large crib for children to run with the freedom to explore the creeks, fields, and forests within the city's limits. Adults also felt secure in this environment; they either knew everyone in town or at least recognized the family names and faces, as many families are multi-generational. Some of the families that immigrated to Bordentown in the late 1800s and early 1900s began businesses that included their relatives as employees of the business. Sons and daughters worked alongside their parents. These situations created a homey atmosphere in Bordentown City — an atmosphere that many didn't want to leave after they *passed over*.

That same feeling exists today. People seek to live here, sometimes waiting until just the right house is available before they buy. Those who are sensitive to it...respond to the sensations that an old home emanates. Many times they are aware that history has taken place here even if they don't know the exact stories. At times, folks sold their houses — only to move into another house in town.

In two of the stories in Part One involving young children, Sue and Lisa are both single women without children of their own...except for the children '*living*' in their
homes. They are completely unknown to each other yet
they both waited to buy just the right house for themselves
in Bordentown City...houses that came with its own set
of little ones.

'Spirit Kids' Run Amuck: Sue's Story...

When I decided to live in Bordentown City, this house kind of called to me. I think it wanted me to buy it. I cleansed the house with white sage, smudging around all the windows. I confidently and continually repeated, "Let all the evil leave this house."

I had a vision of what I wanted to do with the house soon after moving in, but I waited for the house to tell me. I just lived here for three months waiting patiently, listening, and keeping all my senses alert. Then I started to scrape walls, removing the wallpaper. I sensed someone was approving of my choices.

Before long I installed Direct TV. That's when I noticed the activity starting. I would come home at the end of the workday, ready to relax, and the TV would be snowy. The TV was switched to antenna when I left it connected to the satellite. My TV is old. I can't use a remote to change it from antenna to satellite. I have to do it physically, setting up the option: select, select, select. It isn't like a fluke where an airplane overhead will jolt it. It has to be changed physically.

When the TV came back on, cartoons showed on the screen. I'm not a cartoon watcher and it's only me in the house.

One day I said out loud, "I don't care if you want to watch cartoons, but don't take it off the satellite because it's too hard to put it back on. Besides you have 185 channels with forty of them cartoons as opposed to two on antenna." So then when I came home from work and turned on the TV, it would still be changed to cartoons but on satellite. I don't watch cartoons. That's when I did the white sage again. You just never know what's hanging around...left over from an earlier life.

Then it came time to choose colors. I like pale colors. I picked out a light green and a light lavender on the color chart. I folded the sheet so the selections I made were facing up and placed it on the table. The next morning I came downstairs and they were re-folded to a darker shade of the colors I chose. This was early in the morning when the sun streams in through the windows. When I held the strip up to the windows I noticed how good it looked. When I turned the strip over to the first shades I chose, the light colors looked washed out. I went with the colors these *spirits* picked for me. That's how I got these 'Easter' colors on my walls. I finished painting the rooms.

Next I checked the basement. It was all stone and brick and needed to be waterproofed. The kitchen was a later addition tacked onto the house. I had a foundation installed under that too. I wanted that waterproofed also. There are two windows in the front of the house, in the basement. One is small, the other is square. The fellow working on the house said, "Do you want me to fill these in? I can easily cement these up."

"No, I'll use them for cross ventilation when I'm down here in the summer. They're protected under the porch so I'll just make a little screen for them."

The windows were covered with wood and nailed. When I later removed the wood I realized one was a coal chute. "Whoa!" I said out loud. Then I closed that up, immediately thinking I was sorry I didn't have it sealed up. On second thought I realized I could just have the chute taken out and use the opening for a window anyway. I let it go for a summertime project.

The next spring I was in the basement when I noticed spaces between my 'tongue and groove' wooden floors. Some areas were actually broken. If the basement light was on I could see into the cellar. Drafts were coming up through the floor, causing a chill in the winter when I didn't need it. I decided to put some insulation in the basement ceiling. I can do that, I thought to myself, I have a ladder that reaches the ceiling easily.

I happened to be home from work one day when it was raining. I smoke, but I don't smoke in my house. It was pouring outside, so I took my hot cup of coffee at 5:30 in the morning, in the dark, and headed for the basement. It was still spring. I opened the windows, sat down, lit my cigarette, and heard, "Nah, nah, nin-nah, nah," in kids' voices in a singsong way. They were giggling.

"No," I thought, "I can't be hearing what I think I'm hearing." I took another sip of my coffee. I laughed and ignored the sound, knowing my windows were open. Then I heard it again. I came upstairs and looked outside, just to double-check. No one was outside, which I knew, but I had to check anyway. I went back downstairs. I heard it again.

"I know, I know. I'm smoking, but my mother knows and she said it's okay as long as I don't smoke in the house. I'm smoking in the basement only because it's raining outside. Now behave. I'm gonna be home today and working down here. We can have a good time, but you must behave." It seemed quite sensible to talk to the kids.

As I began to work around the basement, I heard and felt "whish" ... like you do when something goes passed you in a hurry. I ignored it. Everything was going along swimmingly. By 2:30 in the afternoon, I was almost done. I was on the ladder, reaching up, when all of a sudden, something that felt like a vacuum knocked me over. I heard nothing, but I felt it.

I tumbled to the floor landing on my hip. Instinctively I knew it was the kids. I yelled at them, "You hurt me. That wasn't nice. You're playing too rough."

I managed to get upstairs to put ice on my swelling left foot. My body was bruised, but my foot really hurt. The swelling alarmed me. It wouldn't go down. So I called the doctor and went to the hospital to find out my foot was broken. I have no idea how it happened. I landed on my hip!

Of course the orthopedic doctor asked how it happened.

I told him the story. He looked at me a little funny. "Well, are you gonna sue 'em?" In turn, I looked at him a little funny. "Duh. They're dead!" He smiled amusingly.

When he returned with the X-ray, thoughtfully he told me. "Well, I believe you. They did a good job. I've never seen anything like this. People break their foot this way all the time and there is always collateral damage. Tendons pulled, something torn. You have none of that. You have a clean break. It'll heal in about a week to ten days because there is no other damage. No muscles pulled. I believe you."

I felt better knowing he believed me.

I came home and talked to the kids. I told them how they hurt me, that I don't mind them being here. I talked to them. Someone told me that once they hurt you they go away. I don't think they left, but I haven't heard anything in a long time. I see shadows, feel movement...and know there is still a presence here. I'm not sure who it is, but I'm sure it's an adult.

Eventually I ordered siding put on the house by some Polish fellows. They talk to the houses they work on. Soon they were telling me they felt something here. How could I resist? I had to tell them my story. While I was telling them about all that's happened, I could see the hairs stand up on their arms.

So that's my story. I think the kids were boys, two of them. Sometimes I wonder if they slid down that old coal chute. I know an adult is here. I don't know who it is yet. The spirits will let me know when they are ready to reveal themselves.

The house? It's fine. Everything works well in the house. I can fix little things that go wrong myself. The house tells me what to do with it. And I just wait to sense it. Now it tells me it's time to re-do the kitchen.

The house was probably built around 1900. At one time there was a big kitchen and bath on the back of the house. I had them removed because it wasn't built to code. The house has beautiful yellow pine floors. I love being here.

Who's Living in Our House?
Gery's and Gerry's Story...

One day a man and his son knocked on our door. They used to live here and wanted to see the old homestead. When we remodeled the house, we brought up the wood floors, replaced the windows, painted, papered, and added a porch along the back of the house off of the kitchen. We also put new siding on the outside, complimenting the exterior with plants and flowers. They were amazed and pleased at the changes. We wondered who else once lived here—and who still does....

Buzzy, our cat, sits at the top of the stairs and watches someone at the bottom. I detect her eyes following that person. It's so obvious that she's watching someone that I can't see. My mother saw the same thing happening at other times and took note of it.

My daughter keeps her bedroom door closed now... after hearing murmurs and footsteps in the hallway when no one was there. At least no one that she could see.

We watch TV with the sound on low. We don't like it loud. That's when we heard the laughter of little girls, it sounded like two of them. So we muted the TV to hear where it was coming from and who it might be. Then we heard a loud crash! We ran up to our daughter's room and she was sound asleep in her bed. Others in the neighborhood have heard children's voices too...also when none were around.

I took a shower one day, and when I came out into the hallway, a brown bag of books that was sitting in the hallway had fallen over. There was no way they could have just fallen over. It was a small pile, not like a teetering tower of books.

One night, after my sister's beloved died following a lengthy illness, her bedroom door opened, waking her out of a deep sleep. There was no wind and no reason for the door to physically open. She knew immediately that he was trying to comfort her. Sometimes you just know these things.

My husband hears someone walking up the stairs, pause, then go down the stairs. Footsteps ... he hears footsteps at times.

He keeps his father's ring that is very sentimental to him in his keepsake chest. He doesn't even wear it for fear of losing it. One day it went missing. With only two of us in the house now, we wondered how that could happen.

My jewelry box opens on each side like unfolding steps. Later when I went to get a pair of earrings from it, a piece of cardboard in it was bent forward. Looking to straighten it, I found his missing ring tucked in there. How?

We spoke of synchronicity and Gery told me this story: My mother and Mary were close friends since early childhood. They were closer than sisters. Mary passed over and Mother was going into an assisted living home. She was a bit nervous and apprehensive. While she was sitting in the doctor's waiting room, his door opened and Tina, Mary's daughter, stepped out. She hadn't seen her for years! Tina comforted her and gave Mother her telephone number. It was like touching Mary. Happenings like this make you wonder if someone is pulling strings for you.

Fred, the Friendly Ghost: Karen's and Rhonda's Stories...

*K*aren and Rhonda both work at the Chiropractor's Office. As they told me the story of Fred and their haunting experiences, Karen and Rhonda spoke at once; as one would begin talking, the other picked up the tale and continued on, both telling the same story.

Ever since we moved our practice to this new location in the summer of 2001, I've had the feeling of someone being here with me in the massage room. I don't always see something, but every once in awhile out of the corner of my eye, I'll see a vision of...half of a woman. I see the outline and details even though it's more of a shadow, not something bright. She is shorter than me and is from the Victorian era, wearing a long, billowy gown. This is her favorite spot. I wonder if she is revealed because of the high energy levels in here.

This is the only place in this building that I see her. I think because it is a calm, serene room. It's more appealing to the feminine.

Sometimes I get a feeling of a man. I've named him Fred. He likes to play tricks with the lights in the massage room. At first we thought it was the X-ray machine, but it happens when the machine is not in use. Then we thought maybe the switch was loose, but our switch is a slide that we keep at halfway. Everything is just as we set it, then the next thing you know, the slide is all the way down. We discarded the idea of a loose switch.

My office is in the back; the massage room is located up front. I'll hear footsteps coming toward me so I'll look up, expecting someone to enter my office. When no one enters, I'll get up and look down the hallway. No one is in there. I also keep my door open, always. It's a pocket door. Someone closes it when no one can be seen. Pocket doors don't blow shut. Then I think...it must be Fred.

Fred also likes to turn the volume up suddenly on the music we have playing. At first we thought it was pro-grammed that way on the CDs. Then we noticed it also happens when the radio is playing. We couldn't find any other explanation for it.

Pencils...Fred likes to play with pencils. I'm often alone here at night. Quiet. No one is about or on the sidewalk passing by. With these big windows it's easy to see no one is outside the office. No one. Then a pencil rolls across the hard floor. It can be eerie when I'm here by myself.

Sometimes I'm in the basement alone because my cli-ents' appointments run past closing time. The desk girl will have gone, locking the door behind her. I'll hear a heavy man's footsteps. I can easily tell the difference between heavy, masculine footsteps overhead and the sound of footsteps coming from the café next door. Even though it's one building that contains both business spaces, a wall separates our basements.

I'll come up the stairs half expecting to see someone, but no one is in the office. I'm alone, except for the sounds of those heavy footsteps. It's always the same footfall. After hearing it over and over again, I can identify it...It's Fred.

There are cold spots in parts of the basement, not areas that are reasonably understood. The basement is tight, no drafts. But walking from one end to the other, I'll walk through a cold spot. It's not the cold of winter. It's different. If I just move away one step it's not cold at all.

I get the impression of a soldier's uniform. I envision knickers and a big hat with a feather. It's a time period before the twentieth century.

The eye doctor that occupied the office before us only used the front portion of the building. The boss renovated the unused space. *(It seems that renovating a property awakens sleeping ghosts.)* He told us that while working late at night he heard the same heavy footsteps.

Lately we've been having a lot more 'activity' going on. The copier machine turns on and off...the heat goes on during the night when it hasn't been cold enough for us to turn the thermostat up. The front door opens and closes. When that happens we think he goes next door. They also have activity and it's the same physical building. Water turns off and on. Sometimes it's left running. Fortunately the sink hasn't run over. We think the increased activity may be from our talking about your *Ghosts of Bordentown* book. Perhaps Fred wants to be remembered in your second ghost book.

I'm glad we have friendly ghosts.

Fred—and Rita? Linda's Story...

After listening to Karen and Rhonda, I went next door to the café to talk with Linda. It's the same building, but divided into two separate businesses. Linda's café is a relatively new business in town.

Linda began telling me her tales:

I began seeing ghosts as soon as I moved into my café. I'm no stranger to psychic happenings...I can draw on earlier life experiences to explain present ones.

This is a very long building, going four rooms deep. The front is the public room or the seating area, the second is the kitchen, the third is the baking room, and the last is a large storage room.

One day when (my employee) Jessica and I were cooking in the kitchen, she said, "Did you see AJ go by?" I told her AJ was in the front.

"But I felt him rush past me. It had to be AJ."

Linda was chuckling at this point. She continued.

I knew when she felt the breeze brush her back as she was concentrating on cooking...it was really our ghost. She just assumed it was AJ.

The other night when I was here alone, I heard my name being called, "Linda." It was loud enough for me to answer, "What?" I turned. No one was here. I had to laugh.

Dishes fall off the shelf when no one is around to knock them off. Shadows and movement are common. I just accept their being here. They harm no one.

When I am cooking here alone, I glance up often to see shadows go by. The kitchen doesn't offer anything that could cast a shadow. I already know what the shadows are, so I don't pursue it. I'm very comfortable with my ghosts.

Once I caught a glimpse of red hair. I feel like it is an older woman. Recently I got into a conversation with a customer who told me a woman named Rita once owned a deli here. She apparently did a lot of baking. I never mentioned my experiences to the woman. It just seemed odd to have this conversation with a stranger at a time when these things were happening. But that is synchronicity for you.

I have never felt afraid with the activity that goes on. Actually, it's comfortable, welcoming. If it is Rita, we both share the love of cooking and baking as we share the same kitchen...just in different time frames. I felt warmth from her immediately.

My staff and I all seem to see the same shadows in the same areas. Though they feel more of a man's presence. We think it may possibly be 'Fred' from next door.

Having different spirits around I can tell one personality from the other. One thing that happened was definitely not the woman...it was too mischievous, more of the man's touch. The last room in the building holds the supplies for the café. The door is always open because we are in and out of there all day long. For a whole week, every time someone went in there, the door would shut and lock behind them. We don't even have a key for that door.

We'd look around. "Where's . . .?" Yup. They'd be in that back room, pounding to get out. I'm glad that didn't go on for more than a week.

Regretfully the Café is no longer in business. But the ghosts had nothing to do with Linda leaving.

The Spectral Family: Lisa's Story...

I don't really consider myself psychic, but I always know what kind of mail is in my mailbox before I even get to it. I sometimes see shadows out of the corner of my eye, movements that my eye catches. But nothing solid can be seen.

The Civil War interests me greatly. I went to Sharpsburg, Maryland where the Battle of Antietam took place. It was the bloodiest single-day battle ever fought on American soil. As I walked the battlefield, I could feel the sorrow weighing heavily in the air. I walked around Miller's Field and around Dunker Church where the fighting raged in 1862. I felt the fear of the soldiers sink into my skin. Maybe my paranormal abilities are a bit developed.

I've worked in hospice for many years. At times I've seen a white mist — not a damp mist that you can see rising from a pond early in the morning — but a thick haze leaving the person as he died.

I grew up in a house that was over a hundred years old on Quaker-settled land from an English grant. I've always been around old things. They bring comfort to me. I love them. I interpret at the Arch Street Quaker Meeting House built in 1693 in historical Philadelphia.

Whenever I visited my friend Patti here, I would wander all through Bordentown, just loving the feel of the old town. The time came when she was planning to get married and move away. I bought her house. It backs up to the old Quaker Burying Ground. I took some time to clean up a few of the old Quaker graves.

I went out one Saturday morning to plant a Pecan tree in a small area where nothing seemed to grow. My shovel hit a solid clunk. It was a coffin-shaped box. I contacted the New Jersey Historical Society. The woman was buried pre-Revolutionary War in 1712. Her last name was the same as this house built in 1850. Maybe a descendent built it. There are many unmarked graves here.

Old houses have their own sounds...if you listen to them.

The walls of my house just seemed to wrap around me in comfort. In my living room, the stairs to the second floor have been altered, changing the direction of them. The stair landing is in the same place flush to the wall that separates me from the house next door. I think at one time this was all one house rather than the two houses divided by a common wall.

My three cats watch, unafraid, as *someone* comes down the stairs. I hear several different walks in the house daily. Children play on the landing. It's very clear and it sounds like two children. I think it's a three-year-old girl and a two-year-old boy. They're giggling and playing with a ball. A family with six children once lived here — two passed over when they were very young.

In the nineteenth century, Bordentown had epidemics of typhoid, cholera and diphtheria. All three diseases were responsible for the deaths of children. The diseases came from contaminated milk that came from unhealthy cows fed with swill and not allowed to roam fields, but to wallow in mud and their own manure. Human contact and dirty water were also factors in spreading the disease. Around 1890 Dr. Henry Colt and Nathan Straus shared concerns over the high rate of infant/children mortality. They both sought to certify raw milk and make all other milk pasteurized.

After living in the house awhile and identifying the sounds I took the time to talk to them. "I enjoy having you here as long as you don't harm me. If you like, I'll release you and that will allow you to join your parents and sib-lings." They haven't gone. I feel as though I've adopted a spectral family. Not scary, though.

I sometimes smell the scent of my father, telling me he is near. He was eighty-three years old when he died. He was an avid glider as I am into flying. When I visit my sister and see a turkey buzzard gliding passed us, I jokingly tell her, "There goes Dad." It's a good feeling when I know he is near and looking after me, guiding me.

The Happy Child: Chris' and Marianne's Story...

Both Chris and Marianne are of Irish descent. The Celts are known to have a strong sense of the 'Other World' and the supernatural. Marianne's mother and grandmother have the 'ability.' She follows in their tradition and wonders if her daughter will fully develop it too.

I first met Chris when he was restoring his house. He saw me coming out of the post office and called me over. He wondered about the old place, asking if I knew any of the history. Of course my interest piqued immediately. Later we got together so they could tell me their story....

Chris began, "I came from living in the country to buy this house in Bordentown City in September of 2003. I met Marianne while I was doing the badly needed restoration before we moved into it. The house was built in the 1850s. It has wooden pegs instead of manufactured nails. Old houses and antiques go together and we love both. We also love living in Bordentown with its great history and great downtown area. It's a special place."

Marianne continued and Chris nodded, agreeing with everything she said.

"From the very beginning when we moved in, there was a strong scent of spring flowers throughout the house. It was a pleasant aroma. Once, we saw a man and woman sitting at the table. A large vase of fresh flowers stood between them. They appeared to be relaxed and just admiring them, soaking in the scent."

Chris picked up the conversation.

"We're both very meticulous about the house and furniture, so when something is out of place or at least not the way we left it, we notice it right away. We usually set the two stools in the kitchen under the counter before we go to bed for the night. It's a neat kitchen to greet us in the morning. But sometimes we come down in the morning to see the stools pulled out and facing each other. Hmmm..."

"I've seen the same thing as Chris at different times. It's a dark shadow of a hooded figure about six feet tall, standing over our bed."

"And I've seen the same figure coming up the cellar steps, too. But Marianne hasn't seen him in that area."

Chris isn't concerned. He takes it in his stride.

"We both see lots of shadows moving about. They don't bother us, they just move around tending to their own business. We catch a lot of movement. That's when we see something out of the corner of our eyes, but we don't actually see anything. But we do catch the movement."

When friends came over for a visit, a solid figure of a happy ten-year-old boy greeted them on the porch, his arm high in the air, waving his hand vigorously. He was wearing a white tee shirt and jeans. Their friends asked, "Who was the kid?"

They just smiled knowing who it was that greeted them.

"Once the boy ran between Marianne and me. I didn't see him that time, but Marianne saw him clearly enough to describe him to me. It matched the boy I saw."

Marianne continues... "Only one time did the boy not respect my privacy. I was taking a much-needed, leisurely bath. I was soaking and enjoying the relaxation. The boy came into the bathroom, paused, then turned and left. It was quite unexpected. He's a happy kid. And I always see him as a solid figure, always in his bluejeans and white tee shirt, never as a silhouette or shadow."

"Another time we heard running up the steps to the third floor. At first we thought it was my daughter. Chris and I looked at each other realizing on second thought, that she wasn't at home just then. We checked. No one was there. The rooms were empty. We're sure it was the boy. He seems to be happy here."

Chris and Marianne finished restoring the house, moved to another larger house in town with more property around it. They lovingly refurbished that house. They invited me to their home for the interview. The second house is exquisite, reflecting their love of home and antiques. But something was missing and now they've moved back into the house they first shared. And share it with others... even if everyone doesn't see the others.

The Jolly Ghosts: Pat's and Frank's Story...

*P*at started telling the tale of their hauntings. Frank filled in pieces here and there.

It started soon after we bought the house, which settled on April 1, 2003, and began to restore it. The house was completely empty. We heard walking in the living room. It sounded like long skirts rustling. We were cleaning and painting an empty house...yet we could hear the steps across the bare floor to the stairway and up the steps.

I wondered if spending so many hours in this old house (it was built ca. 1820) was working on my imagination. Then a few days later my brother stopped in. We weren't home yet, so he drifted out to the back patio to wait for us.

When I did get home he told me, "Something funny is going on here. When I step outside the back door, I hear someone inside in the living room. But when I go inside, the room is empty and I don't hear a thing. Sounds like skirts dragging across the floor. Like the rustling of skirts on those old-fashion dresses. I thought you had come in the front door. But nobody was there. The house was empty."

We checked it out by moving through the door to the back patio. We sat there and we could hear the walking across the floor, the swishing of skirts back and forth.

It took us about a year to complete the house before we moved in. We still heard the walking, but it was a softer sound because we installed carpet.

We moved in and one afternoon Frank was hanging curtains, my brother was here, my baby nephew, my sister-in-law, and me. I stood in front of this small door next to the fireplace. I was showing my nephew these faux books that cover up this cement column. When I opened the door, this mist came right up, went around Frank, and came at my baby nephew and me. My brother tried to catch it on digital camera; I saw the bright flash going off. It went around me and straight up the steps. That's the first time we actually saw the mist. Everything happened so fast. We checked the camera right away, but nothing was on it.

A couple of months later my neighbor across the street told me:

> *"My boyfriend and I were looking out the window when we saw this mist walk from your gate, up the walkway, and enter your house. The door never opened, they just went right through it ... I don't believe in this stuff, but I had to tell you what we saw. It was a mist."*

One summer night Frank was on the telephone talking to his relatives in Venezuela. It was at least eleven o'clock. He heard someone scraping his shoes off near the front door and multiple voices talking quietly to each other. He thought it was some of the neighbors. So he went to the door with the telephone in his hand. The window was open, too. He didn't see anything. He continued talking on the phone when he heard the voices again, this time thinking it must be some folks who just came to look at the garden. We don't mind that, it's okay with us even if we aren't home. So again he went to the door and looked outside. Nothing. He immediately said goodbye, put the phone down, and went to bed.

The next event that happened was the TV came on in the middle of the night. I woke and said, "That's funny I hear the TV." I went downstairs and the TV was on. No one was there. Frank was sleeping soundly.

A short while later some friends from Farnsworth Avenue were here for dinner out on the patio. As they readied to go, we stood in the living room and the door handle, with a tassel hanging from it, started to sway back and forth. We all watched it. I have four witnesses other than us that saw it. We were all stunned.

It seems psychic activity is stirred up more so when children come to visit. On that night when the doorknob turned, our friends' ten-year-old boy didn't want to sit out with us adults on the patio so he was in the living room watching TV.

This past winter (in 2005) during the snowstorm, we could hear some folks right at the door again cleaning their boots on the scraper. You could hear it clear as day. I was on the telephone with my uncle and said, "You would not believe what I am hearing! It's so clear!" He replied: "Maybe because it's an old house, it's a port in the storm and they are just going back to that same scenario. At least they're cleaning their shoes off."

The night we put the Christmas tree up and the Nativity on the mantel, it sounded like there was a party going on downstairs. We heard all kind of 'noise' that night. I guess they were enjoying it.

We still hear them walking through the house. It's not necessarily a bad thing. The first night Frank went to Venezuela (he would be gone five weeks) there was so much noise going on in this house. I don't know if it's because he was gone, but it was crazy! There was so much noise downstairs. It sounded like someone was stomping their feet hard on the floor. The cat came upstairs and got in bed with me. The noise even affected him.

Again, Frank heard three different voices at the front door. Again he was on the phone talking to a friend. "Company's coming. I better hang up." The voices were that clear. No one was out there. I went all over the house, in the dark. I'm not scared, but I would like to see them. I tell them:

"Show me you're here. Then again, I think, maybe you better not."

We'll find the little door under the steps and the cellar door open with no visible hand seen touching them. The lamp is unplugged often. I'll ask Frank, "Did you unplug this lamp?" "No, I didn't do it." Then we know who did. That's pretty much what we live with all the time.

We had a woman with 'second sight' come in the house to see us. She said, "I don't want to alarm you, but there is something in your house. I feel it's a woman and she's friendly. No one to be concerned about."

Frank says: "One morning I was laying in bed thinking, I'll just stay here a few minutes more while I plan all the things I have to do this morning. Go to the post office, stop at the bank — I was very awake. Then the bed was bumped. Really, obviously bumped. It moved. I got up right away."

The Realtor that showed the property to us said that there might be a ghost in the house.

"Is it a good ghost or a bad ghost?" Pat asked him. "He really didn't know and it didn't bother us, so I bought it. We're not scared, but it can be unsettling when there is a lot of activity."

The house now stands on a crowded, tiny street in an intimate neighborhood one block long. But at one time fields and forest surrounded it. It was part of the Joseph Bonaparte estate.

Blessing the Spirits: Filomena's Story...

T he house had a sad feeling about it when I bought it. So the very first thing I did when I moved in here was to have Elsie (Masick, teacher, counselor, and author of *The Warrior Within, A Journey to Higher Wisdom*) come and bless the house for me. She suggested I put a red bulb in the hallway to help with metaphysical healing and for protection of the house. We did meditations and purification rituals. The house took on a much happier presence. And it became a happy home.

Cleansing and blessing the house was important to me. I'm a great believer in the metaphysical. My grandmother and I were born with a veil. My mother and daughter both have a developed sense of psychic abilities, too.

My daughter was three and a half years old when I moved here. She was the first to see the man in farmer pants (bib overalls) and flannel shirt smoking a cigar in the house. She was scared at first, but so excited about it. No one was allowed to smoke in the house! She came running into my bedroom to tell me.

Her bedroom and the kitchen were the only two rooms in the house without carpets. In the center of her room is a very cold spot. It's a small area of extreme coldness, not chilly like a draft and it's always like that even in the summer. I've wondered if that's a vortex where the spirits come through.

Since then I, too have seen the solid figure of the man in bib overalls, flannel shirt and smoking the cigar, too... just like my daughter said. But he appeared to me much later. He looked like a farmer. He wasn't misty or smoky or even a silhouette. He looked like a real person. I could see the blue in his overalls and the smoke from his cigar.

Not long after that I developed a strong desire — a real compulsion — to plant roses. That alone was very strange. I admit that I have never been able to grow anything. Cactus die on me. My thumb has never been green. I cleaned the area alongside the house where an oil tank stood years ago. Huge piles of dirt hunkered there. I prepared it for planting. My rose bushes grew profusely. The six bushes I planted blossomed abundantly and beautifully. No one was more surprised than me! I've since added all kinds of other flowers and they bloom and multiply. Amazing.

We learned later that Gunner, the former owner, grew prize-winning roses in that same area. I'm sure he is the man in the bib overalls.

One night not long after I moved in, I was lying in bed when the door opened. A little girl with dark hair stood there and looked at me. Just looked. She didn't speak or move or anything. Then she disappeared. Just dissolved. I think she was checking out the new family living in her house. I wondered if the little girl was the daughter of Mr. Gunner.

After seeing her resident ghost, this non-gardener compulsively began planting six rose bushes that bloom profusely. The side entrance to her home graduated from dirt piles to a beautiful, lush walkway full of colorful roses. *From the author's collection.*

Friends have been in the house at different times when they catch the sound of children's laughter and running footsteps upstairs. We hear that a lot in the upstairs hallway. "Mommy" is clearly being called. Sometimes there is a cold spot there, too. Not the kind of cold that's normal, but a coldness that isn't normal. It makes me wonder who they were in their lifetime.

Since living in this house for the past twelve years, we experienced items being moved from one place to another when none of us have moved them. I'll lay keys down on the table and later find them on the chair. We see doors open and close without anyone near them. We also watch as the TV goes on and off whenever. No particular time... just whenever. My watch batteries never last more than three months. Telephones don't last more than six months whether I've paid twenty dollars or eighty dollars for them. They go dead and stay that way.

There is sometimes a mist that hangs in the corner where the dining room meets the kitchen. That will happen in the early morning hours or at twilight. I have no idea what that is, but it doesn't bother any of us. So we don't bother it.

When the rose garden was completed our non-gardener spread out to include many other flowers that also continue to blossom and beautify. *From the author's collection.*

Once my ex-husband, a non-believer, came over to break through a wall so we could access the back stairs to the third floor. I wanted him to bless the area and four corners of the room. Often, when a physical area in a house is altered, spirits in the house are disturbed too. The blessing would keep them at rest. As he started working, he saw a white outline of a woman. He didn't hang around to ask who it was. He was downstairs in a flash!

During a sleepover of my daughter's, one of her girl-friends laid her purse on the bed. Then they all came downstairs together. When they went back upstairs, the purse was gone. They looked everywhere for the purse. They tore the bedroom apart, but no one could find the purse. Again they all came downstairs. When they again went upstairs the purse was lying on the bed, in plain view, exactly where she put it in the first place. No one else had gone upstairs. The six girls were always together.

My friend Paul's hearing aid went missing for four days. He takes it out at night and puts it on the night table when he climbs into bed. He finally found it in the center of the bed, between the sheets.

Our basement doesn't extend under the kitchen area. A crawl space is there. One day the plumber came to clean and repair the trap and kitchen sink pipes that extended down into the crawl space. He took his tools downstairs, placing the tools he would need into the crawl space ahead of him. When he climbed into that space, the tools were gone. When he backed out of the crawl space he looked around and saw the tools on the basement space floor. He was a little spooked.

One afternoon I dozed off on the couch. I was in a light sleep, like a twilight zone. I saw a circle of people; some of them were sitting around a table playing cards. It was very smoky. They appeared to be drinking. Since that vision I've been trying to find out how old my house is and if a lounge or business was ever in this location.

I got goose bumps more than once while I was interviewing this couple in their home. As we sat at their dining room table, my knees became ice cold, nowhere else, just my knees. It's my habit to record during the talk as I take notes, but the tape from this interview revealed nothing but a buzz. That's never happened in any interview I've done.

The Maternal Ghost: Mary's Story...

I 'll start with my mother's background. She was born in Perth Amboy, New Jersey with a "half veil," a fine sheet of skin that covered her forehead, eyes, and came down to the tip of her nose. This was a physical sign of her being born with fully developed psychic abilities. The mid-wife that delivered her cut away the skin, but said nothing to my grandmother about it. Instead she took it with her when she left. The mid-wife sold the veil to a sea captain who paid a great deal of money for it. He knew the veil was a lucky talisman.

About a year later the mid-wife returned to my grandmother's house. She was in tears. After confessing what she had done, telling of her miseries during the last year, she asked, "Please forgive me. I'm hoping my bad luck will go away and my life will improve. I'll never steal anything again." With that said, she handed her an envelope, turned, and abruptly left the house. Grandmother, puzzled by all that was said, opened the envelope slowly. She was startled and grateful to find it was full of much-needed money.

So my mother was sensitive to the Spirit world. Growing up in the house she was born in, she often felt someone patting her lovingly on the head. She would turn around, "Momma?" No one was there.

The family was awakened one Christmas by the sound of dishes being thrown and broken in the kitchen. Her older brothers raced down the steps to catch the villain. No one was there, but one candle was accidentally left lit on the Christmas tree standing in the kitchen. It fell and ignited bits of straw strewn around the kitchen floor in honor of the Babe in the manger, a tradition brought with them from the old country in Europe.

The boys extinguished the fire quickly; no harm was done. Not a broken dish was to be seen either.

Mom and her brother Eddie used to 'fly' down the steps from the second floor landing to the ground floor. It was their favorite game, one that they never told anyone about. They would just jump off the second floor landing. Mom told me, "It felt like someone had their hands under our arms and flew us down landing softly at the bottom."

Mom continued telling me her story about flying. "My mother used to scrub a stain on her bedroom floor. No matter what cleaner she used, nothing would get the stain out of the floor. Finally she just threw a small rug over it. A few years later when my brother and I were grammar school age, the police came to the door with a short, balding man. Mother sent us out to play so the adults could talk. That very same night my brother and I were sent to my oldest sister's house to stay for a week or so."

"When we returned my brother Eddie broke our silence and told his friend how we could fly down the stairs. The friend didn't believe him so he came over to watch us. Eddie took his usual leap in the air and flew down the stairs. But this time there were no hands to hold him and he landed with a thud. He broke his wrist on that flight."

The next day my grandmother told them they were moving to Staten Island, New York. She refused to live in that house anymore.

"We heard the reason why as soon as we moved into our new home. The balding man that came to the house with the police confessed to killing his wife and bricking her up in a wall in the basement. He told the neighbors that she left him. The police came and removed her remains from the basement. That's why she sent us children to our sister's house to stay. During the move the area rug was picked up in her bedroom. The stain was gone. The woman's spirit was released from the house."

Daughter inherits psychic ability...

I guess some of that psychic ability was passed down to me. I am 'sensitive' to things of the spirit realm. As a child, when I wasn't feeling well, I would be encircled by a cold, tingling sensation. I just took it for granted that everyone experienced the same feeling. Only later in life did I realize that it was a spiritual, ghostly hug. I'm not sure which ancestor was hugging me, but I do know it was one of them. I think it was one of Dad's that *passed over* in the house we were living in. I feel that in my bones.

Strange things happened to me years later when I married. My husband and I went to upstate New York to visit friends of ours. They lived in a colonial saltbox house built in the 1700s divided into two apartments. The house was on a horse farm where the husband worked for the owner. Jack and Joy lived upstairs; Pete and Ann lived on the ground floor. I was really uncomfortable in that house.

The dining room (it doubled as a guest room with a pull-out bed) was especially dreadful. Jack wanted to show me the hand-hewn beams and handmade nails in the attic room. He knew of my interest in historic houses. I could not make myself walk up those stairs! The sensation of pure evil washed over me so much that I could not make my feet move onto that first step! Jack laughed at me, teasing me with a twinkle in his eye.

I couldn't sleep in the guest/dining room either, not even with a light on all night. I tried closing my eyes, but the feeling of fear filling that room was overwhelming. As soon as Jack left for work in the morning, I crawled into bed with Joy to get an hour's sleep. The overwhelming feeling extended into the rest of the house, too. If Joy ran out to do a quick errand, I sat on the front steps until she returned. I just couldn't deal with being alone in that house.

I never found out what happened in the house, but I felt it was a violent murder, probably many years ago or Jack and Joy would have known about it.

When I met Arlene in her shop in Bordentown, I lived alone, by choice, in my flat in an old house built in the early 1800s. The house was divided into apartments in the 1900s. My landlord, a single man, lived downstairs. At least I thought I lived alone in the second floor apartment...until some resident spirits started to make their presence known.

My earlier experiences told of hard-to-ignore-odors at certain times of the day. The times never varied. Around 4:30 to 5:30 in the afternoon the strong smell of perspiration floated through the air as if a hard working man had just arrived from his job ready to bathe for the evening.

Following that hour the air would fill with a distinctive cherry blend pipe tobacco aroma filling the air. The landlord living downstairs didn't smoke at all. It certainly wasn't mine. The other constant was the aroma of rich, French dark-roasted coffee and burnt toast at eleven o'clock at night in my apartment when no one else was in the entire house.

Living alone in the apartment in a house unattached to another, it's easy to pick up on the habits of others. My landlord went to bed after the eleven o'clock news. He wasn't making coffee. Besides he used the same brand as I did. The aroma I smelled was quite different.

On occasion the waft of camellias floated through the air. It brought freshness to the stale air of winter from closed up windows. It was a pleasant, different experience.

I heard stories about my apartment after I moved in. Debbie, a gal who owned a business on Farnsworth Avenue, had a sister who lived in there before I did. She told me her sister often left a bowl of fresh fruit on her kitchen table in the morning. When she got home after work the apples would be lined up in a row on the table next to the bowl. If there were no apples in the bowl, just other fruits, nothing would be disturbed. She never figured out why.

My friend Donna lived in the apartment next door. She used to do 'commando raids' on my refrigerator while I was at work. She knew there were always some chocolate-coated popsicles in there just waiting for her. Also waiting for her sometimes when she opened the door from the hall to the living room were voices of people having animated conversations. Until she stepped into the room...then there was nothing.

In wintertime, the evening comes early. Before I get home from work, it's dark. I parked in the back of the property because my entrance is from the back of the house. This one time — and only one time — I glanced up to my apartment and saw a blue light glowing from my windows. It was a bright, cobalt blue. Stunned, I just stared. I don't have any blue lights in my place. I shook myself and started up the steps very quietly, creeping slowly, wanting to catch a peek at whoever was in there. Before I got to the door, the light vanished. I walked in — not a soul could to be seen.

Ghosts appear outside, too. One night in January, after New Year's Eve, I was closing the café curtains in my living room. The windows face Second Street looking down to Park Street. Some movement caught my eye. There appeared to be a second story landing on the building on the corner. A door opened, casting light down onto two stories of stairs. There was the landing by the door, the stairs angled to the left, another landing, and then the stairs dropped to the sidewalk. Three men clamored down the stairs, walked to the street, placed their hands on each other's shoulders, forming a line and began to dance, kicking their legs in the air. Two men were white and one was African-American. They obviously were having a grand time. They appeared to be singing, too, as they danced.

I thought to myself, "Those fools are going to catch a death of a cold" because they wore no coats. It was frigid outside. It was then I noticed their clothes. They were wearing white pirate shirts with billowing sleeves cuffed tight, form-fitting dark pants and high boots, folded down at the knee. I was amazed, even more so when they vanished in a few seconds. Poof. Gone.

I also encountered poltergeist activity. My habit was to place my shirt and slacks on the back of the kitchen chair to wear to work, take a shower, then get dressed. One weekday morning, as I followed my normal routine, I came out of the shower to find my shirt missing. I looked everywhere including under the bed. Why I looked under there, I have no idea. But I did. I also did some 'under the breath cursing' before I gave up and wore a different shirt. Two months later I found that very shirt under my bed. It wasn't there the day before when I cleaned.

One spring I was having problems with wasps getting into my kitchen and buzzing through the rooms. While reading in bed one night, I was very jumpy, one eye was reading, one eye was kinda watching the hallway for a wasp. I saw movement. With paperback book in my right hand, I got ready to swat that buzzer. My eyes widened. The movement was not a wasp, but a smallish, slightly built man with gray hair. He wore a dark kind of 'Abe Lincoln' type suit with celluloid collar on his shirt. I saw right through him! He was all black and white with head bowed walking down the hall away from me. I felt an air of sadness about him. I began to leave my bed to confront him...and poof! He dissolved. Thinking about it later, I really believe he was the former owner of this house. My landlord bought the house from his estate. I imagine he built the house and is still bound to it.

The strangest incident that happened not quite to me, but involved an earring. My landlord was sitting at his desk writing checks, and grumbling about increasing taxes along with the other bills he had to pay. Making ends meet, especially with the upkeep of an old house, was tough. Something hit him in the head, slid down his shoulder, onto his lap and fell to the floor. It was a woman's earring! He was struck silent. He lived alone. No one else was in the house.

When I got home from work, he called. "Mary, it's Ray. Would you come downstairs right away?" Ray was white, obviously shaken. "Is this yours?" He held up an earring. I looked it over and shook my head. "No. I've never seen it before." He went through a list of possibilities of how I may have lost it. "Ray, it isn't mine." He told me exactly what happened. This time it was I who was stunned. He handed me the earring saying, "You can have it. If the other one shows up, you'll have a pair."

I took the earring to a jeweler in town. He identified it as mid-to-late 1800s costume jewelry.

Bordentown, being situated on the Delaware River, is a natural home for feral cats. There are many cats kept as pets here, too. My cat story is a bit different from most. There were a number of instances when I was in bed that I felt a small animal, like a cat, walk across the covers and curl up to the small of my back.

One day my friend Sharon called me. She was hysterical. "Something is wrong with Sasha!" I told her to wrap Sasha in a big towel or small blanket and I would pick her up outside her apartment. We drove to the Animal Hospital where they X-rayed Sasha. They found a large tumor on her brain and advised Sharon to have her put down. This wasn't an easy decision for Sharon. She and that cat had been close companions for fourteen years.

We stayed with Sasha, petting her as the doctor gave her the injection until she drifted off. I drove Sharon home.

The next day, as I was driving down Park Street just about where the Divine Word Seminary grounds are, I heard a loud "Meeeeeow!" I jumped. Stopping the car, I pulled to the side of the road. I checked the front passenger seat first because that's where the cry came from. I looked all through the car thinking one of the feral cats we feed on the property had gotten into the car without my noticing it. I wouldn't want it trapped in there. I found nothing. Oh, well. At this point I no longer questioned these things. When I thought about it later, I realized it was probably Sasha meowing her last good-bye.

Needless to say I got to work late. When one of the girls asked if everything was okay, I just said "Yes, thanks. I'd rather not talk about it." You know, you just can't tell people about these things. They don't believe and they don't understand unless it's happened to them.

Another day at work my boss was standing in front of my desk. We were talking while he was sipping coffee. All of a sudden everything became 'super slow' motion. I was stunned. I sat there and watched this strange thing take place, when someone touched my left shoulder and whispered in my left ear, in a man's voice, "Mary, I'm here." I quickly turned my head around. No one was there. When I looked back towards my boss, everything was back to normal.

There were other times, in the car or at work or at home, when I had drops of an oil-like substance fall on my skin or on my eyelids. I have no idea what it was or what it means.

My mother Rose came down from Brooklyn and spent the last few years of her life with me.

One day Mom and I went into Trenton to see an Eskimo artifact exhibit at the museum. We went up to the second floor walking leisurely, looking at all the items being shown. Mom walked in the Eskimo room, checking out the masks, clothing and such. She then turned as she was talking to me. I wasn't behind her. I was clutching the door knob. She later told me that my face was sheet white. I could not walk into that room! I felt pure hatred and an evil indescribable. She hurried back to me, took hold of my arm, turned me around and walked me to the elevator. When we reached the outside we sat on a bench. I told her what happened. She quietly understood even though she didn't get the same reaction.

While Mom was still living at the apartment, I got up during the night to go to the bathroom. Remembering the delicious ham leftover from dinner I decided to have a bit of a snack before returning to bed. I sat at the kitchen table happily munching away on my ham, when a wind whipped through the kitchen! The wind chimes hanging from my ceiling fan were ringing and swaying like crazy. It was such a gust that I raised my arm against it, protecting my eyes. I leaned into it. The force was strong. As fast as it started, it stopped. Dead stillness. The following morning I asked Mom if she heard anything during the night. She didn't hear a sound.

After Mom had her first stroke she slept in the room next to me, separated by an archway. I'm a light sleeper anyway and I would hear a woman's voice softly calling my name, "Mary...Mary..." and I would wake with a start thinking my mother needed me. I'd be yelling "WHAT, WHAT?" Then she would wake up saying, "What's the matter with you? What are you yelling about? You woke me from a sound sleep."

That also happened years later after Mom passed on and my friend Judy shared my apartment for a while. I'd rise from a deep sleep, annoyed at leaving my sleep, and yelling "WHAT, WHAT?" Poor Judy was groggily waking up saying, "What's wrong? What is it?" She had no idea what was happening.

Judy also experienced things. Going to bed at night, she'd drop her slippers with the toes facing outward so she could slip right into them in the morning. When she woke in the morning the slippers were positioned with the toes toward the bed, completely turned around. Also she always lined up her shoes neatly in the room before she went off to work. When she returned home they were scattered all over her room.

Before the Quakers settled Bordentown, the Delaware Tribe of the Lenni Lenape Native Americans occupied it. This area was a crossroad of trails, a meeting place for the gathering of tribes for trade and Pow Wows. The Indians were peaceful and were treated fairly with respect by the Quakers who settled here. The Farnsworths who first bought the land that is now Bordentown City paid the Indians for the land even though they had already paid the English 'owner' for it.

Shortly after Mom *passed on*, I was sitting at the kitchen table writing checks for my bills. The inner door was open, but the screen door was locked as usual in warm weather. I began to feel uncomfortable...like you do when someone stares at you. I glanced up briefly to the entrance to see this 'thing' looking at me. He filled the whole space, shutting out the light from the doorway. He appeared tall and was covered with brown fur with the face of an Indian Wolf Kachina doll. I froze in my chair, heart pumping wildly. I stared at him, he stared at me. Then he tilted his head slightly to the side and...poof, he was gone. It only took a few moments, but it rattled me. I wondered what an Indian spirit/totem/kachina image signified. Was this an omen for me?

Mary lived in her apartment for about twenty years before moving to Florida, where she now battles hurricanes. She says:

"Give me my Ghosties anytime. They weren't nearly as disruptive as these awful winds and rains."

A Ghostly Warning: Charlotte's Story...

My husband Richie and I purchased a house on Chestnut Street that once belonged to a member of the Shipps family. The Shipps were very prominent in town for many years dating back to the mid 1800s. I had already owned the house I live in now and we were living here then and both working. So it was on Sundays that we did most of our moving; moving stuff in and cleaning the new place.

Every Sunday after church, my mother and father would bring my aunt with them to stop in and see us.

One Sunday morning Richie and I were doing chores in the new house when we heard some loud noises. Almost like a roaring sound. We looked at each other! "Where is that coming from?" We followed the sound to the fireplace...my big, lovely fireplace. It captured my attention when we first looked at the property and was a deciding factor when we chose to buy that house. My father followed us into the room, but none of us could find anything that would explain it. Richie and my father went downstairs and looked everywhere. They checked all around the fireplace base, too. Ohhh, it was eerie!

This happened three weeks straight. We could never find anything to explain that eerie noise or find out exactly where it came from. We were pretty sure it was the fireplace, but what would cause that roaring sound?

There was a beautiful library in the house all lined with knotty pine paneling. My mother took a look at it and said to me, "That doesn't look like it's been cleaned for a long time. If you want, I'll clean the paneling for you."

"Great," my aunt chimed in. "I'll do the windows." With that said they both set off to work. My mother was working from the top of the ladder. Suddenly she came down the rungs and cried out, "C'mon, Jim, I want to go home." I was surprised at the suddenness, but I didn't say anything. Everyone has their own way of doing things. My aunt went with them.

The next Sunday the three of them came back while we were still working on the house.

"Did you finish cleaning the paneling?" My mother was looking at me with a funny expression on her face. "No, I haven't gotten in there yet."

"Well, I'm not goin' to do it." Still she looked odd.

"Okay," I answered her, never thinking to ask why. I just didn't give it any thought. I was busy.

"Well, I'll finish the windows," my aunt said. She wasn't in there long when she came out suddenly and nearly shouted. "C'mon, sis. I have to go home. Now." All three left. Abruptly. I noticed, but again was too busy to ask questions.

The following Sunday Richie and I were up in the third floor rooms. One was a big room with a loft. Young Harry Shipps used to sleep up there when his family owned the house many years ago. His buddies from college would come and stay with him, too. There was also a large cedar closet. I was in the cedar closet wiping it down and Richie was in the other room. All of a sudden I heard, "Yo! Yo!" It was a loud shout. I came out of the closet and said to Richie, "What do you want?" He looked at me in surprise. "I didn't call you. You called me. That's why I'm over here." "Are you sure?" "Of course I'm sure."

He paused. "It must be the folks coming in downstairs." We went downstairs and not a soul was in sight! No one! I picked up my cleaning stuff and said, "I'm outta here! And I'm never coming back!"

And we never did go back. We left our paints, brushes, trays and everything else there. I wouldn't go back there for anything. I'm guessing my mother and aunt must have experienced the same thing when they worked in the room with the fireplace and didn't say anything to us.

We came back to this house to stay. I wanted that house so much. It was beautiful. There were French doors that led out to the patio. Everything about the house was special. But, we put it up for sale. It sold quickly.

A month or two later there was a fire in that house. Guess where? In the fireplace, in the chimney, that's where. We wondered if young Harry's father was calling up to him or if a spirit was trying to direct our attention to that fireplace...trying to warn us. We'll never know for sure, but we often talked about those eerie sounds we heard. I'll never forget it, that I do know.

Generations of Psychic Ability: The Author's Story...

I loved my house. I knew the minute I walked through the front door that I belonged in it. It just felt good being there. I also knew it was the end of one chapter in my life and the beginning of a new one. But my story begins way before that day.

I've had moments throughout my life when I was fully aware of my psychic abilities. Mostly I ignored them. To begin with, I didn't know what to do with them. So I just took notice. If I wasn't under pressure at the time, I wrote the experience down. I have no idea why I did that, but I did.

Mom never talked much about her youth or family. I was married with children before I knew that my grandmother, Elizabeth Urbanski Daniels, was born with a veil on her face indicating fully developed psychic abilities. It was then also when I learned my mother, Anna May Bice Riggi, had extraordinary psychic abilities where her children were concerned.

My first-born son possessed it too.

My son Kenny came racing into the kitchen one hot summer afternoon. He had been playing outside with his little friend Mark. He was about six or seven years old. "Mommy, Daddy's on fire!" I knew his father was in the bedroom sleeping. To reassure him that everything was okay, I took him by the hand to peek into the bedroom. To my surprise the electric extension cord to the air conditioner was sparking flames! Surely my son saved his father's life.

Several years later my marriage crumbled into a battleground. In the middle of the night I left my husband of fifteen years and took my four sons and my widowed mother with me. I went directly to my bachelor brother's apartment, interrupting his calm existence. I'm sure he must have been horrified, but he never said a word other than welcome. I began to plan for a future.

First he helped me get a job. Then he helped me search for a house. I was determined to live in Bordentown City. Their excellent school system drew me in, especially for my youngest dyslexic son.

These things were not easy to do, considering my lack of a high school diploma or a credit history in my own name. This was 1972 when the average woman rarely got credit on her own merit. The newness of my employment was also a factor. Each weekend we looked at houses in the price range I could afford on my new salary. The location of the first one was ruled out. The second one was tiny and located next to a firehouse—not suitable. The third didn't feel right. The fourth needed too much work to be comfortable. An apartment was ruled out. No one would rent to me with four children. I was becoming dismayed. I couldn't impose on my brother's generosity much longer.

Finally, someone told him of a house tucked away on a tiny side street in Bordentown City. It was the only house on the street. It was an old one. The location was perfect, away from the center of town and a stone's throw from a forest and Black's Creek. The home we left behind was also near a wooded area and the boys spent as much time there as they could manage. I wanted to provide the same type of area for them. Boys need room to explore and have adventures.

My brother Bob contacted the real estate office and set up an appointment for early Saturday morning. We met the realtor at the house. The front door brought us directly into the living room. It was small, but cozy. Straight ahead on the left were the steps to the second floor. Across the room on the right I took a step down to a pleasant dining room. On the right was the bathroom, unusual but acceptable. On the right also was a door leading to a screened-in porch. Across that room and another step down led me into a large kitchen. Bright yellow. Not modern, but sufficient with lots of cabinets and scalloped woodwork trim. Beyond the kitchen, through a wide archway, was a dining cove wrapped with windows. The sun was bursting through the windows casting cheerfulness over the room, a promise of happiness.

I just filled with joy picturing all of us around the table being a happy family again. I agreed right then and there to buy the house. "This is it. This is home."

The salesperson laughed. "You haven't seen the second and third floors yet."

"I don't have to, but to make you happy, let's go."

I looked at the front bedroom, which would be mine. The tiny closet was the old-fashioned kind where you hung your clothes on a peg. It was easy to see people didn't own much in the way of clothing when this house was built. They were the days of a dress for Sunday and one for the week.

The two front windows overlooked a quiet street. It wasn't wide enough for two cars passing; one would have to back down the street. Next were two steps down into the back bedroom for the two younger boys. This also had a small closet. The bright sun shone through the large window that overlooked the roof of the breakfast room. Perfect for bunk beds. Along the interior wall was the stairway leading up to the third floor and a neat hide-a-way room for the two older boys. This room sported a sloping ceiling, giving it an interesting look. It reminded me of the attic in the house I grew up in, except it was a lot smaller. I loved that attic and now this one, too.

Mom would want the dining room converted to a bedroom. She wouldn't have to climb stairs for the bathroom located off the living room. That was a little inconvenient, but easy to live with. The rest fit perfectly.

The paperwork went smoothly. We settled in.

When I left my husband, I had only the clothes I was wearing. I had nothing else. Friends were very generous. They donated odd bits of furnishings to us, even books, toys, and clothes for the boys. I began to rebuild a life.

My newly acquired day job, working in an office Monday through Friday, paid the bills. On Friday and Saturday nights, when the boys were visiting their father, I tended bar at an old historic tavern in the countryside. This was for the extra money that was always needed. It was a busy schedule. The boys, ages seven to thirteen years old, were all in school. My mother was there to help out and was home when the boys came charging in the door, hungry after a long day of being confined in a classroom.

On the weekend nights that I worked, I would get home about three o'clock in the morning and sometimes later. Tending a busy bar was no easy feat. And we were always busy. It was fun, too, but I was standing, and sometimes running, on a tiled concrete floor for six hours straight. The bar and dining room were usually packed with thirsty patrons. When I got home sleep came quickly and soundly.

One Friday night or Saturday morning really, I awoke from a deep sleep. It must have been about four o'clock. Standing just inside my bedroom doorway was a little girl. She stood about three feet high and looked to be six or seven years old. Her hair was fair, long and curling at the ends. Her little toes peeked out from under a floor length nightdress and a nightcap with a ruffle around it. She held a flickering candle with a bright flame. A pensive but pleasant expression on her face seemed to be telling me that she was checking out the new family now living in her home.

Without speaking a word, she conveyed a welcome to me. She approved. Then she just disappeared. Just faded away. Just dissolved.

I was bone tired, but I was comforted. I fell back to sleep.

When I awoke the next morning, I thought of the little girl immediately, before I even placed my foot on the floor.

I lay there thinking about her and decided not to say anything to my mom. I didn't want to frighten her or be ridiculed as to having a dream.

So I said nothing to anyone. After all, the appearance of a spirit in one's bedroom could be the beginning of a lot of innuendoes and jokes about my condition when I went to bed. I was tired, but I knew what I saw and I also knew that I didn't have to explain it to anyone else.

Mom's Story...

My mother, Elizabeth Urbanski Daniels, was born with a veil on her face. This means that a thin piece of skin covering her complete face at birth had to be cut away. Folks in the know say this means the person is born with a fully developed second sight.

Family stories tell that Mother was known for having saved more than one life because of this gift. The story most repeated in the family tells of her reading tarot cards for a friend living down the block from us. In the middle of the reading, she burst out, "Gracie, hurry, hurry, run home, quickly. Your house is on fire!"

It was. After it was all over and everyone was safe, Gracie found out that her young son was experimenting with matches when the curtains in the kitchen caught on fire. The neighbors doused the kitchen fire and the baby sleeping in the second floor bedroom was safely removed. No real harm was done. Luckily for the neighbor, Mother's warning stopped what could have been a fatal disaster.

I struggled for years keeping my family together. I raised three children while my husband was in the hospital fighting a terminal disease that eventually took his life after seven years. Money doesn't come easy when you don't have an education for a decent job. I love my children, so that made the years of hard work worth it.

Like my mother, I also have a highly developed extrasensory perception, but only where my children are concerned.

I moved to Florida after my children were grown and out on their own. By that time, my first grandsons were about three years and one year old. My daughter and I stayed in touch by telephone and letters and cards—her letters, my telephoning. I don't like to write.

After a few months of being a Floridian, I called her and stated, "You're pregnant again?" She replied, "What makes you say that? I don't think so." I knew it before she did. She delivered another grandson nine months later.

It became a tradition for my son Bob to go to his sister's house every Wednesday for supper. One particular Wednesday evening, I called. "What happened? Why didn't you call me? Did Bob have an accident? Is he alright?"

They were relaxing over a cup of coffee after dinner when a loud crash in front of her house had them running to see what happened. Some guy ran into my son's newly bought and highly treasured Cadillac. He worked hard and long to buy that car. This all happened only five minutes before my phone call.

Ten years later, after I was widowed again, I returned to New Jersey and then moved to Bordentown in 1972 with my daughter and four grandsons. My daughter works two jobs to keep the bills paid. She works hard. I make dinner and do the laundry. Our house is old, but it has a nice feeling to it.

My habit is to get up early, around 4:30 in the morning, to have a cup of coffee and start a load of wash. This gets done before they all come down for breakfast, searching for homework, looking for lunch money, running off to school, and to work. A lot of commotion goes on. One particular morning, the strangest thing happened to me. I didn't want to tell my daughter because I didn't want to frighten her.

As I was bending over the washer, I looked up to see a little girl about six or seven years old standing a good eight feet from me. She had long fair hair, curling at the ends. Her little toes peeked out from under her floor-length nightdress and her nightcap had a ruffle around it. She held a flickering candle with a bright flame, watching me, but with a pleasant expression on her face. Not smiling, just a contented, sweet look. I was stunned. I stared. I blinked. She was gone.

I overheard Mom telling our neighbor about the incident. She was afraid to tell me thinking it might frighten me. She was completely surprised when I told her that I had the same experience and saw the same little girl. We laughed over trying to protect each other.

Audrey's Story...
(relating to the Author's Story)

My late husband and I lived on West Street when our daughter was born. Soon after, he stopped in at the deli on Farnsworth Avenue where he ran into another resident, Lillian. We both have known Lillian all our lives.

"Do you know of anyone who wants to rent a house?" she asked him. "Yes, me," he replied. And that's how we rented the house that the author bought years later.

My daughter was about a year old, time for her to have her own room, when we moved into the house. She had so many toys that my mother suggested I place half of them in the attic with the idea of switching them every six months. Then I would take her up to the third floor and, while I was sorting the toys out, she was playing with this little children's phonograph. Instead of playing a record on it, she took it apart. She loved taking things apart and putting them back together again. Once in a while, she wouldn't be able to find a space for a piece that was supposed to go back in. We always said she was going to be a lady mechanic when she grew up.

One particular day, when I was sorting the toys and she was playing quietly, I suddenly felt the hairs on the back of my neck stand up. I felt a presence standing behind me looking over my shoulder. Almost like a coolness on my back. I brushed the thought from my head.

"Mommy," she said with a bit of surprise in her voice. "What?" I replied, lifting my eyes to hers. She said nothing more, but was staring past me, as if she saw someone standing in back of me. I watched her eyes move as though they were following someone moving...but no one except my daughter and I were there.

I didn't say anything to anyone about it. My husband pooh-poohed stories about ghosts or spirits. He just chuckled at me. But then one day, he went into the attic to get something. When he came downstairs he had a funny look on his face. I noticed immediately. "What's wrong?" I asked. "Nothing, nothing," he replied. I didn't press it. He would tell me when he was ready.

A week later he said to me, "You know last week when I was in the attic? There's something up there. I could feel this chill down my back, like when you have a fever and a breeze hits you. I could feel it, but I couldn't see anything. There's something in that attic. I know it. There is something there."

I chuckled. Now he believed my stories. There was never anything frightening or scary, but there was definitely a spirit there. It's funny how the non-believers change after they have the experience of it happening.

Not long after the incident in the attic, our family gathered together for a Thanksgiving dinner. An in-law of my sister's, Mrs. B., I called her, told me that two psychics, sisters, lived in the house for four years before we moved into it. That same afternoon, Mrs. B. told me the house was haunted. Never anything mean or evil or even bad, she said. "Nice ghosts" is how Mrs. B. referred to the many stories she knew of the house. She died some time ago and took her stories of the house with her. But not before she told us things happened downstairs too.

We wanted to buy that house, but we just weren't ready when it was available. I loved that house. Thirty years later, I learned that others experienced something in the same house.

The Ghostly Painter: Audrey's story continues...

Some time after we left there, my husband and I bought a house of our own.

My daughter came in one day and said, "Dad, did you start to paint the back porch steps?" "No, I will eventually, but haven't had time to start any repairs yet."

"Well, come here. Someone must have started to paint them red. Why would anyone paint steps bright red?"

We all saw it. It wasn't really like anyone took a brush to it, more like a splash of red. Streaks. Then we thought no more about it. A couple of days later, I went out to hang clothes on the line. I didn't notice any difference on the way out because I was carrying the clothesbasket. However, on the way back into the house, I noticed the step was clean. He must have found something to clean the paint off, I thought.

When he came home for lunch and I asked him, "What did you use to get the paint off the steps?" "I haven't touched the steps yet. I haven't had time. Why?"

It was gone. The steps were clean. The stain was gone. When my daughter came over, I showed it to her.

"Daddy's playing a trick on us," she said. "The steps are immaculate."

He swore he didn't.

Six months later, it was back — the bright red streaks were back. They were in the exact same place. This time when friends came to visit, we showed the spot to them so they wouldn't think we were kooks. Then it disappeared... but later it came back again. I suggested painting the steps, maybe a different color. My daughter got a bad feeling about that. "Please don't do that, Mom."

So I didn't. We never did find out what it was.

My husband died. He always said he would come back in his next life as a tiger.

With my husband gone, I put the house up for sale. In the meantime, I rented the house out to a couple with a teenage daughter. I told them my husband was very sick there just before he died. Some people are squeamish about those things, so I told them right up front. They had lived there for a short while when they called me. "Did your husband work at night?" "No," I told them. "He worked for the city, daylight hours, 7:30 to 4 o'clock."

"Every night at 10:30 on the dot, I hear what sounds like a lunch pail being dropped onto the table. I thought it was your husband. His ghost is in this house. I feel he is still in this house."

They also heard noises coming from the semi-detached house next door. A family lived there for a while. Then it became empty. They insisted the noises continued after the house became vacant. They even checked to be sure no one was camping out in there illegally.

My father was psychic, too. He was ill with Parkinson's disease in his later years. During the week, I drove my daughter to school, then went to visit Dad and help my mother with him. She had a bad knee and couldn't do it all herself. On a day when I was needed for some extra activity in my daughter's classroom, I telephoned Mom not to expect me. I would be spending the day at school. I didn't want my father to be disappointed waiting for me when I wasn't going to be there. When my mother tried to tell him not to expect me, he insisted that I would come to visit.

"She's going to be here, you'll see. She's going to call. You'll see." She ran out of patience with him when he kept insisting. Well, my job at school didn't take very long after all, so I telephoned to say I was on my way. "I told you," he said.

He often sensed just before the phone would ring. And it would ring. Mother used to marvel at it. I can do that too. Sense when the telephone is going to ring. I don't know how, I just know.

Now, years later, I've remarried and live on a different street in Bordentown City. The first day we were moving in, a tiger cat came to my back door as though he belonged here. I wondered about that thinking of my first husband. But my new husband built a beautiful house for the cat to stay in at night. It even has indoor/outdoor carpeting in it.

Tiger's litter box is in our bathroom. It has a large lid that screws onto it. Once I found the lid removed and under the window. There are only two of us in the house. I didn't do it nor did my husband. So who did?

Sometimes I get a little depressed, who knows why? But one such day I was feeling blue and thinking, 'I need a sign of some sort. Something to tell me God is real.' I was carrying a pile of folded clothes upstairs. When I came down, my favorite poem given to me by my daughter had fallen off the wall.

It didn't fall straight down like you would think. I looked around the bottom of the steps. Nothing was there. The wind was blowing in the open windows and door, but nothing else had blown off the wall where a lot of my pretty things hang.

Puzzled, I looked further away from the stair area. Then I found it. My favorite poem was flat under the dining room chair where I always sit. I also keep my pocketbook there leaning against the legs of the chair. Now I was even more puzzled. There is no way this wood-framed poem could have blown off the wall without breaking or have gotten flat under the rungs of my chair. I checked the nail; it was secure, not even loose. No one else was in the house.

The poem? "Footprints"... the background is a sandy beach with footprints on it. It says that the Lord is with us even when we don't realize it.

'The Lady' Who Never Left:
Jackie's Story...

I grew up in Bordentown City. My grandmother lived in a huge house on Farnsworth Avenue. I loved that house as a child. Nana was bedridden most of my childhood, but she would always have a treat or a quarter for me when I visited her. Her daughters, my dear aunts, would host wonderful parties and dinners there for the family and sometimes for friends, too.

My mother adored her mother-in-law, so she and my dad bought a house on Elizabeth Street. I could walk to St. Mary's School easily. Bordentown City was a wonderful place to grow up. Everything was within walking distance — the movie theatre, two soda shops, the Delaware River for swimming and boating, and the pond for ice-skating.

My husband, Larry, grew up in Georgetown, only six miles away but definitely country.

When we were first married, we rented a home in Bordentown City, but bought our first house in Mansfield Township, which was definitely the country to me. It was a lovely ranch-style house, but became too small for our growing family. I started looking around for a bigger place.

I yearned to be back in town again. My Aunt Peg told me about a house that was just around the corner from her. It was a large, six-bedroom colonial that was built in the 1700s. It had been vacant for several years and in dire need of major repairs, but I fell in love with it. The second I stepped into the center hall I knew I was home.

The dining room had windows on both sides of the room making it light and airy. The doors in the room were painted black. Knowing I couldn't live with black doors, we tackled the dining room first. We primed the doors and repainted them white. We wallpapered the walls and the room looked charming. Shortly after, the doors were streaked red. I assumed it was probably a chemical problem and promptly returned to the paint store. They had never had a problem of that sort and offered little help. So, we sanded the doors and repainted. Shortly thereafter, strange red steaks reappeared. Over the years, we repainted many times and the streaks always reappeared. It took a lot of years, but, eventually, they disappeared. However, they were always a lively topic of conversation when we had dinner guests.

Our youngest child, daughter Vicki, was two and a half years old when we moved into our historic home in town. Shortly after moving in, she developed an imaginary friend. We would ask, "Who are you talking to?" She replied, "I'm talking to the lady." Being the only girl in the family with three older brothers, I thought she created the friend for some female companionship. Over time, I've re-thought this. The *Lady* certainly made herself known to all of us as well.

In the middle of a winter night, I was awakened with a gentle nudging to my shoulder. Opening my eyes, I saw an apparition of a short woman in a white nightgown with a high ruffled collar. She appeared to have curlers rolled in her hair. The figure stood by my bedside waiting. I pinched myself to see if I was truly awake. She moved swiftly across the room and out the door. I have no idea why, but I climbed out of bed and followed her into the hall. I no longer saw her, but I smelled smoke! I raced downstairs to the kitchen where I found a pan in flames on the stove! I screamed out for Larry! He came running down the stairs and quenched the fire.

My brother David lived with us at the time. He was heating up some leftovers and fell asleep while waiting for his food to get hot. It got hot, that's for sure.

I told Larry about the woman in the white nightgown. He excused it as an intuitive dream. I knew I was awake, I wasn't dreaming.

My father, too, fell in love with the house. Instead of enjoying a leisurely retirement, he took on the job of renovator. My husband was delighted! Dad and I worked together wallpapering, sanding floors, and remodeling. It was a labor of love for both of us.

Eventually Dad and Mother moved in with us. A six-bedroom house can accommodate a lot of people. One weekday I was doing chores around the house while Mother watched her 'soaps' on TV that she loved so much. After running the vacuum all around downstairs, I headed for the den. Since Mom's show was still going on, I plugged in the vacuum, but sat down to wait for the show to end. Ten minutes later the vacuum leaped to life! We looked at one another. Mother commented, "I think your *Lady* is impatient."

My mother had a green thumb. Their large bedroom on the second floor was full of plants. It looked like an indoor garden in there. One day, while she was watering a hanging plant, she glanced out the back window and was lost in thought when she felt a gentle touch on her shoulder.

She later told me, "A feeling of tranquility flowed over me. When I turned around, the room was empty. I was the only one I could see."

Mom passed away shortly after that day. My father and I did everything we could to keep her plants alive, but we were unsuccessful. I often wonder if the *Lady* was trying to tell her that she and her plants would soon be going to a better place.

Our family and many of our guests have heard footsteps up and down the stairs, felt cold blasts of air and...felt something in the house. We all became accustomed to the lights going on and off unexpectedly. However, when my children were teenagers they delighted in the gasps and screams from their friends when this phenomenon would occur.

I loved to throw dinner parties and set a beautiful table in the dining room, but more often than not people always ended up in my kitchen. My cousin Jane and her husband Malcolm and their family visited often. Malcolm was a definite disbeliever when it came to anything ghostly.

One evening they were sitting at our kitchen table and I was preparing something at the counter with my back to them. All of a sudden I heard them both gasp and jump up.

When I turned around there was a stream of water on the table. "It squirted us, but it came from nowhere!" They both bawled at once. "We don't know where it came from!"

Malcolm quickly became a believer.

My family and friends just welcomed the *Lady* and accepted her as part of the family.

After a few happenings I became curious to know who she may be. I knew the Herron family lived in the house next door in the 1800s. Their son, Dr. John Herron, became a veterinarian. When he married in the early 1900s, he bought the house next to his family.

That's the house we bought.

I went searching. I knew Dr. John's daughter, Joan, lived in the area. When I talked with her, I described the *Lady* to her.

"That's my mother! She always wore her hair in tight little curls piled on top of her head." "Did she die in the front bedroom?" She sounded surprised at my inquiry. "My mother moved to California after my father, Dr. John, died."

Looking back now, I remember that soon after we first moved into our house, the house next door to us was rented to a young couple. The couple became a family of three. During the night the new mother went downstairs to heat a bottle for the baby. As she climbed the steps to the baby's room she saw an apparition of an old woman in a white nightgown at the top of the stairs. The mother screamed and ran for help.

The next day the parapsychologist from Princeton University agreed that the house was haunted. That same day the young family moved out.

Fortunately for all of us, we welcomed her. After our children were grown and began their own families and a new grandchild was expected, we brought out the cradle to set it in the corner of the room. At times it rocked gently with no hand seen touching it. The lady has been a part of our family for many years and certainly a part of the house. She apparently loved it as much as I do.

The original part of the house was built in the 1700s. I just loved it and I'm very grateful my children grew up in Bordentown City.

Brother David's Story...

My mother had several heart attacks and was unable to do a lot of things she was used to doing. My sister Jackie took on the responsibility of taking her shopping, doing her housework, and washing the laundry. It was an extra load of work for my sister, especially with four children, but she did it gladly.

My dad was retired, but working on renovating her old house. He and my mother were at Jackie's house more than they were at their own home. After talking it over we all agreed that a good solution was for Mom, Dad and me to move into the big house. It would be easier on Jackie, with only one house to tend. I was nineteen at the time.

I moved into the back bedroom on the third floor. The front bedroom was empty because the three younger children were sleeping in the big bedroom across from mine until Vicki's front bedroom was finished. My sister kept the hall light on all night because the stairs were steep and there was no bathroom on our floor. She wanted to be sure the children could see if they needed to go to the bathroom during the night.

One night my door opened and a burst of light flowed into my room. I looked up to see a short figure in a white nightgown. She quickly turned and left the room. Thinking it was Vicki sleepwalking and fearing she would fall down the stairs, I jumped out of bed and saw her move towards the front of the house and turn right into the front bedroom. I quickly followed and entered the room. It was empty! Totally empty! I went to the children's room and Vicki was fast asleep in her bed. She wasn't sleepwalking after all.

In time I came to know who the person was roaming the house at night wearing a white nightgown and looking after all of us.

My brother, Jim, was married and living nearby. We would frequently spend the evening together in town. On our way home he would stop in for a bit. One night we were sitting across from each other at the dining room table enjoying a warm fire after the chilly walk home. A loud noise resembling a whistling kettle came from the closet.

Jim asked if I was going to investigate. I looked him dead in the eye. "No way!"

He simply said, "Good night." And left the house.

I went upstairs and went to bed. Later I learned he told his children never to enter our house unless they saw Aunt Jackie first.

Son Robert's Story...

I had just passed my ninth birthday when we moved to Bordentown. We had been living in a small ranch style home on an acre of ground. The first thing I remember about our new house was the huge center staircase. Coming from a house all on one floor, it was now exciting to run up the stairs, slide down the banister, and do it over and over again. My brothers and I hardly ever walked down the stairs.

My bedroom was the smallest. It was located on the second floor to the rear of the house. We believed the room was much bigger when it was originally built in the 1700s, but was divided in half when indoor plumbing was installed.

I almost learned to accept having my bedroom and closet doors open and close by themselves. Many lights would go on and off by themselves. Most of my family took these things for granted. I had some reservations.

When I grew up, I moved to Florida. I came home for visits to hear more ghost stories from the rest of the family, some of them new. We would have a few good laughs at the storyteller's expense. On one of those visits, I was awakened by a strange noise from the closet. It sounded like a whistling teakettle. It got so loud that I had to leave the room! Mom came down early in the morning to find me sleeping in the den. When I told her what happened, she told me about her two brothers and the 'Night of the Whistling Teakettle.'

I had never heard that story before, but now I knew, first-hand, exactly what my uncles experienced.

Son Jay's Story...

Growing up in a house where spirits are present always makes for lively conversations. Our home was always full of family and friends. Most of our family and many of our friends have personal stories about our ghost. The description was always the same: an old lady in a white nightgown.

Although she didn't appear to everyone, she made her presence known in different ways.

Lights flashing on and off, appliances starting unaided, unexplained noises, and objects moving about or even disappearing. It became so commonplace for us to discuss these occurrences at home that I started to talk about it at school.

Of course there were the skeptics. So one day I took the Polaroid picture of the old lady sitting next to my sister into school with me. My peers were interested, but so were my teachers! Ghosts were the topic of conversation for several days at the high school after that day.

When my girlfriend (now my wife) was in college, she took an extra year and went to France to study the language. She wrote me letters and sent cards all written in French. Not knowing the language myself, I would wait for her to call and translate.

After receiving one such card I stood it up on my dresser to await her phone translation. That night my bedroom door opened. I immediately got a freezing cold sensation across my chest and couldn't move. The old lady walked across the room at the foot of my bed. She went directly to the card, lifted it from the shelf and then gently replaced it. She then turned and left the room. The room was still freezing and it was awhile before I could move.

Of all the ghostly experiences we had, that was the most intense for me.

Daughter Vicki's Story...

I was the youngest of four children. Having three brothers born before me, one would expect to grow up in a spirited environment. Ours was more *spirited* than most.

When I was about four years old, my grandfather bought a new Polaroid camera. He was getting familiar with it by taking pictures of us all while still sitting at the dining room table after dinner. He was holding one of the photos in his hand watching it develop. A very strange look came on his face. He kept looking down at the photo and then looking to the opposite end of the table where I was sitting.

Finally, he murmured with an inquisitive look on his face, "Who's the old *Lady*?"

Sure enough, sitting right next to me in the picture was an old lady with her hair in tight little curls. She was wearing a white nightgown.

We've had many ghostly stories over the years, but that picture memory is my favorite.

Our house was always full of family and friends. Every Sunday during football season my mother would cook early for all of us. My father is an avid Philadelphia Eagles fan and there was always rowdy conversation with any of our friends who chose other teams as favorites.

On one such Sunday when I was a teenager, my brother's girlfriend and I were in the kitchen alone. It was late in the evening and we were making snacks. She was mixing tuna fish salad and I was pouring sodas. We heard footsteps approaching from the dining room into the kitchen. We looked up to see who it was, but no one was there. Then the back door opened and closed as if someone left the house. At that point the girl was mixing the tuna fish so rapidly that the tuna was flying everywhere. The next thing we knew, we were hugging each other and getting out of the kitchen.

After I got married, we took an apartment in Borden-town Township. When our first child was on the way, we bought a house in need of extensive repairs. My parents invited us to move in with them until the work was done. We moved into my old bedroom on the third floor. It was going to take a few months for all the work to be completed. Unexpectedly, the renovations took longer. It was obvious we would not be in the house before the baby was born, so we began buying baby furniture and setting it up in the adjoining room.

One night my husband and I heard the baby swing-handle cranking. We went into the room and the swing was swinging away. No one else was in the room at the time.

Anchored to His Home?
Jane's Story...

Bordentown began its history on the water when it was known as Farnsworth's Landing. Trade and travel use on the Delaware River set the beginning of what eventually became a town of shipbuilding and seamen of all classifications. Early settlers navigated on the Delaware River before there were passable roads, only Native American trails. During the Revolutionary War in 1777, Captain John Barry received orders to sail the Continental frigates the Effingham and the Washington along with several other vessels to hide them in Crosswicks Creek. He sank the ships as the British approached. The skeletons of some of these boats and ships can still be seen at low tide in Crosswicks Creek.

Commodore Charles Stewart elected to live in Bordentown during his brilliant sixty-three year career on the sea. Captain Edward R. McCall's commendable lifetime service in the USS Navy earned him a gold medal from Congress for his actions during the War of 1812. He was born in Charleston, South Carolina, but he chose Bordentown as his homeport until he died in 1853.

Shipbuilders were drawn to the desirable location of Bordentown on the Delaware River. Joshua Lamson built two schooners that crossed the Atlantic Ocean by 1852. Both were still in service thirty years later. He went on to build 123 more vessels by the time he retired in the 1900s.

D. S. Mershon built many sloops, schooners, and other sailing vessels before he was commissioned by the United States government to build two gunboats for action in the Civil War. The first was the Cimarron gunboat *and the other was the Mingo. His grandson graduated from Bordentown Military Institute in 1891 and from the Naval Academy in 1895. He served honorably in the Spanish-American War, Russo-Japanese, and became Chief Engineer of the Pacific Submarine Telegraph. He made commander at age thirty-two and went on to become Captain.*

Ships of all sizes, uses, and designs filled the Delaware River along the Bordentown shoreline. Where there are ships, there are seamen, sailors, captains and commodores. Many houses in Bordentown have been homes to sea captains and those that sail under them.

Jane's story begins:

We were a young married couple and living in this house in Bordentown City when I became pregnant with our son. With the pressures of pregnancy, I often got up during the night to go to the bathroom. One night, early morning, really, I got up out of bed as I usually did and headed for the bathroom.

Half asleep, I groggily reached in to feel for the light switch—and... and... and—standing right there was a really tall man. His arms were folded across his chest, like a man looking over a situation. He sported a long pointed beard and was wearing an old-time sailor's suit. A very stern expression covered his face.

I was stunned! Without another thought, I ran back into my bedroom and awakened my husband. He grumbled, but got up and checked the bathroom. Nothing! No one! I just didn't know what to make of it. I have never seen him since that early morning.

That was a long time ago now. When I think back, it's as if he were just letting me know that he was there. Weird.

From time-to-time, we felt a coldness about us, especially going up the stairs. The coldness would follow right on up with me. There was no draft from anywhere, and it didn't feel like a draft kind of coldness anyway. It was different, just this coldness hanging about you. We couldn't imagine an explanation for it, so we just adapted to it.

Many times I heard footsteps in the hall or on the stairway, but when I looked, no one was there. Mostly it was the hallway where we felt that coldness and heard the sounds of someone walking.

Other little things happened. My husband and I noticed the lights going on and off with no one clicking the switch. The two of us would be sitting on the couch with no one else near. We could see no hand near the light switch, but the switch would go on and off like a child experimenting with it. We just looked at each other, not knowing what to say about it.

That's all been a long time ago. The lights work now, as they are supposed to work, and the coldness is gone. Things aren't moved around either. They stay where they are set down in any area of the house. I guess our 'spirit' is finally at peace.

But years ago, when our daughter was a youngster, she noticed that things moved around all the time. She wanted the third floor for her bedroom. I heard a lot of comments from her.

"Mom! Where's my jewelry box? Why do you move my things around?"

My daughter would be yelling but, of course, I hadn't even been in her room. She thought I was snooping because this would happen often with different trinkets of hers. I'm not sure if she ever believed me.

Someone to Look Over Me: Debbie's Story...

*D*ebbie has someone with her all the time. She shows up as a mist usually standing behind her in photos taken of her. She also manages to see that Debbie picks a winning ticket just when she needs it most. Some call it luck. Debbie knows it's something more. She's also proficient in working with Tarot Cards for herself.

Debbie picks up the story:

My husband died a few months ago (before our interview). He kept saying that our Sammie (Samantha), the Yorkshire terrier, was just waiting for him to die. She was. She died shortly after him at seventeen years old. Bill was seventy-five.

There's a lot about life and the after-life that we don't know about. The last days of Bill's illness when he was here at home, his bed was in the dining room. The dining room looked like a hospital and his medicines lined the shelves. I kept a small chair over by the stair steps for me to use.

Word came to us that Bill's brother, Louis, who was eighty-nine years old and living in Arizona, was changing a light bulb, fell off the stool, and broke a hip. During surgery, they lost him, his blood pressure bottomed out. The doctors brought him back. He was in a coma when we told Bill about it. The following day, his brother Joey, my friend Judy, and I were sitting with Bill. I started to sit on the small chair by the steps.

Bill said, "Don't sit there." I looked at him, "Why can't I sit there?"

"Because Louis is sitting there. Are you blind?" There was no one in the chair, but no one could go near that chair for three days. Then Bill said, "Where's Louis?"

"I don't know. It's not my day to watch him."

Bill kinda chuckled, "He's gone."

About two hours later, Joey called me from Delaware. "You're not gonna believe this, but Lou's daughter Patti just called me from Arizona. Louis is awake and out of his coma after three days. Louis told her, 'I wasn't in a coma...I was in New Jersey with Bill.'"

Not believing what she heard, she asked, "Okay, describe what Bill's room looks like." He described the room exactly including the red, white and blue patch quilt bedspread.

The house was always crowded with friends and family during the last few months of Bill's life. Now he's gone and so is everyone else, I'm alone but I don't feel alone. I don't know who it is, but at ten o'clock every morning someone turns on my TV. I've called the electronics people and the cable people. No problem is found. The water faucet goes on too. Somebody is here with me and letting me know it...but it's beginning to quiet down this last week or so.

Debbie took a lot of photos when she lived next door to me in Bordentown. Many photos were taken of her also. A hazy mist could be seen floating around her or vaguely formed in the photos she took. She still takes a lot of photos and recently several were taken of her. The hazy mist still shows up in both style photos.

I asked, "Do you have any idea who is in the photos with you?"

"No, but whoever the spirit is, she came with me. She's here with me. When we dug the pond, she was in the pictures. When I planted the irises, she was here. Actually, my son complained. He asked me to take a clear picture. I would if I knew how."

Guessing that it's her grandmother who raised her and passed over around 1978, we talked further and realized that the mist began appearing when Bill's health first started to fail around 1997.

I've seen several pictures of Debbie right after they were taken. Her mist was standing behind her or off to the side rather like she is overlooking her. They show very clearly what Debbie describes. I've also seen the images of the Indian and the Hessian. The rest of the photos are buried somewhere in boxes still unpacked from her move to her new house. With Bill being so ill she had been unable to take the time to completely unpack everything.

Debbie continues her story.

I'd really love to know for sure just who it is. I never get the chill some people talk about. For me it's a comforting, peaceful feeling. I do sense that I must stay along the Delaware River. I don't know why. But she was with me in Bordentown and has come with me to my new house.

Debbie's protective spirit shows up in photographs as a mist. She's either in the photo with Debbie or in the photos she takes. Courtesy of Debbie.

Skeptics say the film is defective or the camera mal-functioned, but it happens all the time — with a dispos-able camera and even with the digital camera that doesn't use film.

The Photogenic Spirits...

In October of 1999 I took a picture from the river point-ing to the Camden & Amboy Railroad Bridge, I reversed the negative and a Native American showed up in the trees, in the picture. He was in full dress. I spoke to John Mahon about it. He knows all about local Indian history. He told me the Indians always did their spiritual, healing and death rituals in October.

On that same day I went to the Bordentown Yacht Club to take a photo. When I reversed the negative, the image of a Hessian soldier was in the trees. The Hessians occupied Bordentown during the Revolutionary War in the 1770s. They weren't welcomed at all by Bordentonians.

I take pictures at Holy Assumption Cemetery and re-verse them and come out with angels in the clouds in the sky. One day I took a photo of some headstones, reversed it, and a perfect angel appeared.

My niece Casey Marie is an old soul. She had long conversations with my father when she was a toddler. Yet she was born six years after he passed over. She can tell you things about him that is impossible for her to know. Once she told me that she was driving the truck down by the river with him. Her mother used to do that. She couldn't have known that at the time. She thinks he still lives in my dog, Buddy.

The Eerie Basement: Juanita's Story...

My good friend Juanita was tall and slender with flaming red hair. She always appeared wearing bright colors, a clue to her vibrant personality. She was a talented, well-known artist and probably taught art to at least one person from every household in Bordentown. In 1986 she bought the old 1886 Citizens' Hook & Ladder Firehouse on Walnut Street and turned it into her residence, studio and classroom. It seemed everyone knew and adored Juanita.

Occasionally we went out for dinner. With a chilled martini in hand, she began reminiscing about her youth. One of her stories goes like this:

Mother died while I was still very young. Father worked odd and long hours on the railroad. My brother was several years younger than me, so I had to look after him. He was my responsibility.

We had two sets of grandparents that were very different in their personalities. Sometimes we would stay with the town grandparents and sometimes we walked out to stay with my township grandparents.

At this point Juanita paused, looking into a distance that I couldn't see. I knew she was looking at scenes from her childhood, so different from the other kids that she knew.

My township grandmother was a plain, hard-working woman and tried her best to make me into that image also. No silliness or frilliness was allowed when we were there. Then I came to my town grandma and she would dress me with bangles, bracelets and brightly colored clothes. Music always flowed through the house and there was always lots of laughter there. It was a happy home and I loved being there.

In the spring and summer, when we were in town, grandma warned us about staying away from the gypsies camping on Mill Street along the edge of the woods. I snuck up close enough to peek at their bright dresses, belts and bandanas. I heard the tambourines filling the air with music while they danced around the campfire. I saw no danger, but I didn't get too close either.

The only part of staying at my town grandma's that I didn't like was when she sent me to the basement for potatoes or onions or whatever vegetables were in cold storage. I felt creepy down there. And I hated the coal bin. It just emitted an awful feeling. I didn't want to tell Grandma I was frightened. But finally one day, I did.

Grandma then showed me a spot in the basement that never dried. No matter what they did, this wet spot always returned.

The kitchen door that led to the basement was troublesome also. It sprung open even when it was latched properly. It would just pop open and stand ajar. I thought Grandpa was playing a trick on me, but it happened when he wasn't home. It worried me sometimes. It was the strangest thing.

Finally Grandma told me a man hanged himself down there.

Research turned up the fact that one Sunday morning a man did hang himself in the coal bin. That was after he slashed his throat, nearly severing the head, and his one wrist. An enormous pool of blood lay at the base of the chopping block with the razor in it. The basement had a dirt floor. The man was generally known in the city, liked and respected, and reputed to be a hard worker. A carpenter by trade, he was also despondent over lack of work. He lived with his brother and his seriously ill sister. She was sick for a long time and he had been taking care of her.

The life of a home centers in the kitchen. Perhaps his spirit was trying to come back into the comfortable place it once knew. Or perhaps he was just wandering like a lost soul, not being able to cope without work to fulfill his life. Not everyone has the ability to face life's problems and find solutions. But it's sad to end a good life this way.

A Reassuring Presence: Betty's Story...

I was sitting with Betty in the living room of the Victorian house she bought a few years ago. This is the third house in Bordentown she has owned since I first came to know her in the early 1970s. It has a wide, side-entry hallway with a door on the right that leads into the living room. There is also a door that opens to a formal dining room behind it. To the left of the dining room is the kitchen, now very modernized by Betty's talented sons. The house is at least a hundred years old. The former owner was a highly respected scholar and internationally acclaimed genealogist.

Betty is a very creative, talented person. She owned a women's casual clothing store, a tailor shop and gave sewing lessons. Her business, the Pincushion, was located on the main street in this old historic town. She would often be working there from ten o'clock in the morning until after midnight.

This is her story....

When I had the shop on Farnsworth Avenue, I was so overloaded with work between my sewing class, running the store, and doing alterations that I asked Linda to come to work for me. Shortly afterwards, things began to happen. Items were moved, lost, and then found in obvious places. I'd be cutting out a dress pattern, lay my scissors down, get up to go to the bathroom, return, and the scissors would be gone. Looking all around and not finding my scissors I'd be annoyed, go get a cup of coffee, return to my seat, and the scissors would be lying there.

Often when Linda and I were sewing late at night, I'd get up to make a pot of coffee, and come back to our worktable to find the spool of thread I was using could not be found anywhere. Linda affectionately referred to the little events as "Martha's" doings.

Martha was playful, never destructive. When she moved an item I was using, it would be found easily. It was as if she just wanted some attention paid to her.

The time came when I had the opportunity to sell my house in a residential neighborhood and my commercial building on Farnsworth Avenue to move to this house I now live in, still in Bordentown City. I could combine both home and business with lower overhead. I jumped at the idea. Once I made the decision, things went quickly. The last night before the big move, I was alone in my shop thinking about this big change in my life. With change there is always adjustment. I couldn't go without considering my spirit friend...so I extended the invitation.

> *"Martha, it's time to go. You can stay here with the building if you like, or you can come with me."*

Betty paused in her talk and got up to make a fresh pot of coffee. Soon I could smell that wonderful aroma wafting in from the kitchen as the sound of coffee percolating filled the quiet moment. She returned and continued with her tale.

I settled into my new home and set up my sewing shop in the large finished basement. Soon buttons left lying on the sewing table would be found under the cabinet. A yard of delicate, pink silk material necessary to finish a dress I was working on would be stuck in between bolts of navy blue wool. I knew then that Martha had chosen to come with me. During a quiet moment when I was working alone, I heard the sound of a woman's light step walking overhead in the hallway. No one else was in the house at the time. It was kind of reassuring to have Martha with me.

While our renovation was in progress, my son was laying concrete in another section of the basement. He was finishing the floor, sprinkling it with water, working it, etc. He reached for the trowel, and that quick, it was gone! Martha was obviously back to her old tricks and having some fun. He looked around and found it on the windowsill behind some bottles.

Betty paused again, went to the kitchen to pour coffee for us. Returning to the room she said, "The coffeepot was turned off, but it's still hot. I think Martha wants us to know she is here."

Then she continued her story....

Once I searched for an entire week for a jar of salve left in the sewing room before I found it on the second level of the house under the computer. Sometimes while I'm watching television, I'll hear "whoosh!" Down the hallway toward the kitchen, "whoosh!" I know Martha is having fun in the hallway racing around.

I've never really seen her. Once a friend came to visit. We both fell asleep while watching a television program. Suddenly, I awoke hearing a noise in the kitchen. I slowly crept to the dark hallway, down the hall, and reached the darkened kitchen. Carefully I slipped my hand around the corner and flipped on the light switch. No one was there. But the disposal unit was going full force and the switch was still in the 'off' position.

Ghosts Are Knocking: Sam's and Kathy's Story...

Sam and Kathy came into possession of the big Victorian house known today as the Swift Mansion around 1986. It's a quiet neighborhood on a highrise above the place where Crosswicks Creek and Black's Creek enter the Delaware River. The street ends at the corner of their property. The house itself dates back to the 1800s.

Sam begins their story....

Soon after moving into our new home we would hear noises. It sounded as if someone was rapping on an outside back door wanting to enter. We looked, but no one was there. What really confused us was the location of the knocking sounds. There wasn't even a door there. There was a large floor-to-ceiling window like the one here in the front of the house. After researching the history of the house, we found that where the window is now had once been a large wooden back door.

I had four antique lead toy soldiers, which I placed on the mantel of the fireplace in the music room. One by one they were beheaded. I found them still standing upright with their heads broken off and placed neatly at their feet. After the third beheading, and absolutely no explanation for it, I placed the remaining soldier in the china cabinet in the dining room. This soldier's head remained where it belonged. On his shoulders!

Our treasured collector's plates in the same china cabinet were all lined up to face the room. These were turned sideways...but not by either of us. Never broken or chipped. Just turned sideways as if they had been placed differently in another time, in another cabinet. Time and again, I would turn them to face the room... time and again, they would be turned sideways.

When we moved in, we brought a lovely grandmother clock with us. It had been a family heirloom and had always kept perfect time. It stopped the day we moved into the house. Of course a repairman got it working again. As soon as the man left, walking out the front door, the clock stopped again. It hasn't worked since.

In time, our foster daughter, a teenager, came to live with us. She chose the third floor as her room for the privacy that teenagers seek. Soon after, she heard footsteps come up the stairs, across the hall—and... and... and—down the stairs. No one was ever there. Many times she was the only one at home, no one else was in the house. Yet the sound of the footsteps continued.

One evening after dinner, my foster daughter and I were in the living room, my wife Kathy was in the kitchen cleaning up the dinner dishes. Lovely concerto sounds permeated the air. We all ran to the music room to see who was the accomplished pianist. No one was there. The music ceased as soon as we reached the doorway.

Finally, December 25, Christmas evening, after a long day of family reunions and visiting, we came home to quietly enjoy our own living room. It was just the two of us, looking forward to a quiet hour or two...but not for long. As we started to relax, we heard sounds coming from the dining room. Glasses were clinking. We heard laughter, music ... the sounds of someone giving a dinner party. When we reached the doorway of the dining room, we found silence. Not a soul, not a sound, not a movement.

These occurrences and many others took place in the first four years we owned the house. In the fifth year, we had a daughter. Since that time there has been only one brief episode.

But the clock still doesn't work.

House of Her Dreams — Pete's Story...

One afternoon Victoria of Asbury Park, New Jersey walked into Shoppe 202 Antiques on Farnsworth Avenue. She got into a conversation with me and began telling me about her dreams.

> *"I see a grand house in Bordentown. Horse-drawn carriages pull up in front of this mansion. Ladies and gentlemen, very elegantly dressed, step out and enter the house. There are a great many dinner parties going on. Music floats through the air."*

I showed her the stack of Bordentown prints we have for sale. She looked through until she came to the Swift Mansion.

"This is it! This is the house I've been dreaming about!" I told her to go down to talk to (the author).

She continued with her background. "My great-great grandmother, Minnie, was a cook at the Bordentown Military Institute. I've heard stories about Bordentown all my life, but I've never been here before."

The house known today as the Swift Mansion was originally built for Robert Schuyler van Rennssalaer. He was descendant of Patroon Renssalaerwyck of Amsterdam, the most powerful family in the world of the sixteenth and seventeenth centuries. Their international business, which dealt in diamonds, pearls, and other fine luxury items, was called "The House of the Dutch West Indies." The family was extremely wealthy and influential in world trade. They sent the younger members of the family off to different countries to maintain commercial control. A few of the American branch of the family were personal friends of George and Martha Washington.

Robert was born in Claverack near Hudson, New York. He didn't take to the family business of trade, but came to Bordentown to fill his position as Superintendent and

Civil Engineer of the Camden & Amboy Railroad in 1845. He became a prominent member of Bordentown and of the railroad, maintaining his position with them until it was leased to the Pennsylvania Railroad in 1871. He continued to live in Bordentown with his wife, Virginia, until his death in 1877. Because of his family and position with the railroad, they would have entertained lavishly and often. It was probably the Van Renssalaer's horse-drawn carriages that Victoria saw.

George W. Swift, Jr. and his wife Stella (Saylor) bought the house in 1901. They made several changes and alterations to the house. An elevator was installed. He was an inventor holding many national and international patents, becoming best known for his design and invention of machinery for manufacturing.

They also were very prominent in town and very social. He was an officer of the Bordentown Banking Company. Aside from his inventions and manufacturing, he also built the apartments on East Union Street. When the need for a public library arose, the Swifts donated $10,000 to the fund. They were very generous with donations to local and worthy causes.

Unfriendly Housewarming: Phil's Story...

Many years ago my wife and I bought a house in Bordentown City. We were very excited about the house and about living in town. It took a little organizing, but we wanted to move in and place our furniture and things in an orderly fashion so we wouldn't start with a jumbled mess in the house. We carried in and laid our carpets down first. The oriental carpet went into the living room in front of the fireplace.

Then we started to bring in the furniture. As I carried in the next piece, a small neat pile of ashes on the oriental carpet caught my eye. I was curious, but I was busy, wanting to get all of our things into the house. I just cleaned it up and continued to make trips out to the truck and carrying our furniture into the rooms they belonged.

On the next trip in I set a heavy, cherry wood chair in the living room. Before I came back with the next load, the chair was very neatly turned over on its side. The pile of ashes was back on the oriental carpet in front of the fireplace. "Hmm, something's odd here," I thought to myself. But there was too much to do and I was too busy moving our things in to give it too much attention. I turned the chair upright and cleaned up the ashes, thinking no more about it.

After we settled in, a tinkling bell that was sitting in our china closet often woke my wife and me at midnight. We thought that was unusual but not harmful. The cherry wood chair was repeatedly turned over on its side. We never heard the clunk of the chair being turned over, but it would still be turned over just the same. We thought that unusual, too. Not harmful either, but it can be annoying.

Once in the middle of the night, I woke to a heavy weight on my chest. I was alarmed, but my wife rather pooh-poohed the whole idea. Then the next night it happened to her. This was becoming serious.

We felt it was time to call in a parapsychologist. He explained some things to us. "It sounds like you have some poltergeist activity. This means physical materials are moved by mental thoughts. It is not always intentional. Stress, hormonal peaks and mental turmoil can create situations. Often a teenager will subconsciously act as a magnet, especially if they are stressed. They do this subconsciously, completely unaware that the happenings are being caused by them. Females seem to be more susceptible at this age than males."

He went on giving us more information on our experiences, "This is called psychokinesis or PK for short. It is the ability to bend spoons, cause dishes to fly across the room with no apparent reason, levitate a glass of water, etc. Many studies have been conducted on intentional PK. In the case of poltergeist activity, it is unintentional."

He took a deep breath and continued, "You have a teenage daughter in the house. She's probably under stress with moving into a new neighborhood. With caring, time, and understanding, the activity will stop."

We cared, took the time, and learned to understand what was happening. The parapsychologist was absolutely right. The activity stopped and we enjoyed our lovely home in town.

Inheriting the Rituals: Gladys' Story...

lorence became a bride at the approximate age of forty. Her new husband, Cornelius, built a house especially for her. She lived there with her many antiques around her for fifty-four years surpassing her husband's death in 1953. Uncle Charlie worked for Florence for many of those years. Having no heirs and no relatives when she died, she left the house she loved and all the contents to Uncle Charlie. He didn't want to live alone, so he invited my family and me to share the house with him. We all delighted in our new home.

Uncle Charlie and I were always very close. We had a special bond between us. As a child, I helped him by pulling weeds, carrying the ashes to the curb, and other small chores that would lighten his workload a bit.

After we settled in, I continued our old routine. In the spring and fall of every year, we went into the attic and brought down the change of curtains, bed linens, etc., for the oncoming season. Uncle Charlie showed me exactly how he liked things done. I, as always would go along and just do things his way. I also took on the housekeeping. When I ran the vacuum in the living room, I picked up gray hairpins. The next day, when I ran the vacuum again, gray hairpins would be at the same place. None of us in the house had gray hair, so I was curious how they got on the carpet that I just cleaned.

My older daughter chose Florence's former bedroom as her own because it was near the bathroom. "Mom, it's the strangest thing. I wake up and hear sounds of someone brushing their teeth." *(After Florence broke her hip, she always brushed her teeth in bed.)* "I hear a voice in the bathroom saying, 'I just don't understand. I just don't understand.' The voice sounds very dazed...like the person is confused."

Time passed, the children grew, and Uncle Charlie died. He in turn left the house he loved to the family he loved.

After we buried Uncle Charlie, I soon noticed the fan-backed Windsor chair that stood near the doorway to the kitchen was turned to an angle. I straightened it to face the living room. In the morning, it was turned again. Again, I would straighten it. In the morning, the chair faced the wrong way again. This little ritual went on for about ten days until the chair finally stayed where I placed it.

About three weeks after Uncle Charlie was buried, my daughter came home from a date with her eventual husband. Just inside the doorway they heard, "I'm in here. I'm in here." It was Uncle Charlie's voice just as clear as when he was alive and calling her name in the same exact way.

When it came time to do the semi-annual visit to the attic, I asked my husband to help in Uncle Charlie's place. I planned to continue the routine Uncle Charlie set so many years ago. While sorting out the curtains we heard, "Over here, Gladie, over here."

Uncle Charlie was there just as he always had been, calling his favorite person by her pet name. But that was the last time. He must have moved on after he saw me doing things the same way he taught me.

We never heard from him or Florence again.

The Mischievous Ghost: Lois's Story...

O ur house dates back to 1878. A few families have called this home. Surely some of those folks have stayed here and not crossed over as expected. We're living proof of that.

After my husband and I married, we moved in with his parents and stayed. Our two daughters were raised here too. As a family, we've been here for forty odd years...Odd in other ways, too.

It's been awhile now that my mother-in-law passed on, but I often get the scent of her and I see a shadow from time to time. I know it's her. We were always a close family with three generations sharing the same house. We were four generations here for a few years.

When my young daughters were growing up, they got blamed more than once for things they just didn't do. My mother-in-law and I thought they were mischief-makers. When they were both still less than eight years old, their grandmother yelled up the stairs to their bedroom located on the second floor in the back of the house.

"Stop that dancing around and making such a racket!" Then I'd yell up the stairs to them. There was no response. The noise continued. Finally I went up the stairs and down the hall to reinforce their grandmother's command. The girls were in a deep, sound sleep. They looked like angels. Silence filled the room. No signs of anything astray. Or of anyone else being there. Yet we heard the noise coming from that room. Who could explain it?

The girls told me that during their growing-up years, they often felt a cold whoosh of air go past them. This happened in different areas of the house, not necessarily in any particular spot. But in one location in the girls' shared bedroom, they saw an illuminated glow of a man's face on the wall. They weren't frightened. By the time this happened, he was familiar and they were accustomed to his antics. They named him "Andy."

It never occurred to any of us to be afraid. Our ghost was never harmful. Mischievous at times, yes. Items in the house disappeared, and then reappeared, sometimes in the same place. Sometimes we found the items in another part of the house completely unrelated to where we left things. The girls would be accused, but often they were in school or outside the house playing with friends.

One night my husband and I were watching TV in our room at the top of the stairs on the second floor. Over top of the TV program we heard the sound of firm, heavy footsteps coming down the hall to our door. Then they stopped. Curious, I got up went to the door and opened it, not a soul was in sight. No one could disappear that quickly, if anyone was there.

Time moved on. The girls grew up. One day my one daughter was engrossed in a TV program in the living room when tables started to move and bounce around. Annoyed, she yelled: "Andy! Get out of here... out, out!" The front door flew open and whoosh! Silence. After that day, there was never another problem in the house. There was never another thing out of order. No items were lost or misplaced. Unexplained footsteps were no longer heard. No loud noises rang throughout the house when no one was there. The house became normal and dull without the unknown guest that lived with us for so long.

What I thought was forever, wasn't. He's back....

We lived several years without him, but again we're finding missing things placed back into the same place. We hear the footsteps again. And times when I am alone in the house, I hear muffled conversations with no explanations. I hear someone calling me when no one is near. At times when the house is empty, I feel a presence that I can't explain, but I sense it. Someone is here that I can't see...but I can feel it.

During the years my little granddaughter lived here she occupied the same back bedroom as her mother did as a child. She often spoke of the little girl who wanted to play with her.

It's been a happy house for us and apparently for some who lived here before us. They don't seem to want to leave. I can understand that.

Research found that, unknown to the girls, a red-haired, blue-eyed Andrew lived in their house for many years before their family did. He was born in 1873 in Sweden and came to America to join his brother and sister-in-law. He was just twenty years old when he set foot on American soil. He married Maggie, a girl from Ireland who arrived here in 1888. They had one daughter. Andy went to work for the Pennsylvania Railroad, eventually becoming a Signal Forman for the Trenton area. His record shows that he personally walked every mile of track from Mauch Chunk (now Jim Thorpe), Pennsylvania to Trenton, New Jersey; from Trenton to Camden; Camden to Point Pleasant by way of Mount Holly; Bordentown to South Amboy; and Monmouth Junction to Sea Girt. It went on record that the signals were in the best form under his watchful eye.

Andy signed onto the draft for World War I. After the war he became treasurer for the Bordentown Memorial Fund, planning to erect a memorial onto the island on Walnut Street. They collected $2,253.50. Then six months later the committee needed to use $172.94 of the donated money for the cost of moving the memorial seventy-five foot forward in front of the post office to accommodate the fire apparatus of the Citizens Hook and Ladder Company next door. The Firehouse Art Gallery fills that building today. Andy was also a volunteer member of that firehouse and served as vice-president.

World War II began. His wife passed. At seventy years of age Andy became part of the Local Defense Council in Bordentown City.

He had a jolly side, too. He was known as a happy-go-lucky guy ready to laugh at a prank or cause one to make others to chuckle. Andy downed many a beer at Toots'n Reds Bar on Farnsworth Avenue where old friends gathered to share a joke or a story. He spent many an afternoon at one of his favorite pastimes, the horseracing track. In 1936 the newspaper noted that Andy started celebrating his 63rd birthday with a mackerel breakfast. His many friends celebrated the day with him.

Andy passed over in 1965 after enjoying a long productive life. His daughter passed in 1993.

Part Two:

Historical Haunts

The Clara Barton Schoolhouse: Patti and Rob's Story...

*E*ducation has been a major part of the foundation
essential to the growth and development of Bordentown from its early history. This little redbrick
schoolhouse was built in the 1700s. The early Quaker
settlers taught their children here. Private schools were
entrenched within city limits, and by the 1800s, students
were traveling to Bordentown schools from around the
world.

Public funds were given to schools conducted in pri-
vately owned buildings. In 1839 the city leaders moved
the little red-brick building from the corner of Farnsworth
Avenue and West Street to the corner of Crosswicks and
East Burlington streets. Now they wanted to offer free
education to students. The first attempt failed.

Then in 1852, Clara Barton, a New England school-
teacher born on Christmas Day, arrived in Bordentown
with a friend from Hightstown. She was appalled at the
youth lingering in the streets. Her inquiry about the school

system resulted in the town fathers' giving her permission to teach at the school.

Six boys showed up to attend class and helped her with scrubbing and cleaning it. A blackboard hung on both sidewalls. Ms. Barton brought all her own supplies including books and a globe. It was a meager beginning. By her second week of teaching, fifty-five children showed up to learn. At the end of the first year six hundred students registered for the next semester.

When the school re-opened in a new, larger building in 1853, the town hired an outside male educator as principal at twice the salary Ms. Barton had received. Discouraged, she left the teaching profession in 1854.

More than ten years later Clara Barton came upon many of her former students when she walked the battlefields of the Civil War. She held some of them, wounded or dying, in her arms. "The Angel of the Battlefield," became her byname as she founded the American National Red Cross.

The school children of New Jersey collected money in 1921 to restore the little red-brick school building in her honor, continuing the close relationship of children to Clara Barton's schoolhouse.

Over the years, paint has been donated and painters have volunteered to maintain the little building until the present, with the Bordentown Historical Society accepting ownership and vowing to keep it as a reminder that before 1852 and Clara Barton's presence in Bordentown, not all children had access in learning to read and write.

Patti and Rob began to tell me what they have experienced at different times and during the same night in the original Clara Barton Schoolhouse while we sat inside the schoolhouse.

Patti begins....

My story goes back to the late 1990s when the Board of Education owned the schoolhouse. I got the key from them because I always saw people peeking in the windows. They gave me permission to show the schoolroom to visitors. These were usually tourists and the building was always locked. I feel this old schoolhouse stands as a symbol to our modern education today and should be available for all people to see.

The interior of the Clara Barton Schoolhouse was restored to the way it looked when she was schoolmistress there. The painting in the far corner is of Ms. Barton. Restoration and remodeling seems to awaken dormant ghosts or spirits. *From the author's collection.*

The door was seldom opened, so the room was full of dust and dirt, as you can imagine a rarely used room would be. My first thought was to clean it as Clara Barton did 150 years ago. So I came in here, cleaning stuff in hand. I left the door open so fresh air could flow in.

As I began to clean I saw a flash go past the windows. More than once. Movement. It made me a little nervous. Unsettled. A bit scary. I shut the door, locked it, and left. When I got to the Garden Tour meeting the next day, I said, "I'm going to clean the Clara Barton Schoolhouse on Saturday. Does anyone want to help me?"

At the time I thought I would never come back into the building again. Especially alone. Then all week I was thinking about how those first six boys helped her clean up this room so they could learn to read and write. I began to relax.

On Saturday I did come back and clean. Again I left the door open. I kept seeing this movement flash past the windows, like someone running around the building. That's impossible to do because the picket fence is against the brick on the one side. No one could get through that space...but I kept seeing flashes, flashes, and flashes. I ran out to see if any kid was playing tricks, but no one was ever there. I knew no one could run around the building, but I checked anyway. At first it made me edgy, but then I kind of got used to it. Now when I leave the building and lock up, I say, "Good night boys."

Then I stumbled onto a quirk. When I closed the door, nothing happened. When I left the door open, the flashes went past the window as if kids were running around during recess. Now I'm sure that's what I'm seeing. The picket fence wasn't here in the 1800s. It was probably all dirt outside. This area certainly was rural in those days.

I've been seeing this, but never told anyone about it until after this past Christmas Rout (of 2006).

In the second half of 2006 restoration began in the little schoolhouse. The deteriorating walls were re-plastered. The cast iron stove/heater was repaired and new wiring was installed expertly so it can't be seen. The candles in the windows are on timers, but set the tone of days past. Items Clara Barton used or would have used are placed around the room. The benches are period. Personal keepsakes of hers are scattered around. The two rooms upstairs were next on the list to restore. Now it was time to open the schoolhouse for the Holiday Rout. The Rout, sponsored by the Bordentown Historical Society, is a tour of historic houses and buildings usually offered during December. It's one of their fundraisers. I act as hostess at the schoolhouse.

The exterior photo shows the picket fence close to the schoolhouse, making it impossible for boys or anyone else to run around freely. The fence was not there in Clara Barton's day. *From the author's collection.*

Rob and Patti both talk about the night of the Holiday Rout in December of 2006.

Rob begins....

My wife, her mother and I went on the Holiday Rout. We arrived at the schoolhouse while Patti was still speaking about Clara Barton and her impact on early, free education in New Jersey. We listened in and lingered after the group left. Barry, another volunteer, was telling us of the restoration recently completed and what project was next on the list. The second floor badly needed work. That's where the teachers slept.

I was looking up at the opening and saw movement. I looked more intently. Barry's flashlight moved around and glanced the ceiling and opening while he was talking. He was looking away, but I saw a little boy on his hands and knees peeking out. He had blondish hair and was wearing a Buster Brown type of suit with a white shirt. He made eye contact with me, flipped his head back, and disappeared. It was like, 'oops!' As if a typical little boy got caught peeking when he wasn't supposed to be. His face wore an expression of surprise.

I didn't want to say anything, but I thought to myself, "I think I've just seen a ghost." I didn't want to freak anybody out so I edged over to Patti. With her knowledge of the school she may be able to tell me something.

"Has anybody said anything about anybody that isn't supposed to be here or …" I looked at Patti. She mumbled, "What, do we have squirrels now?" She had a weird expression on her face and said, "I'll talk to you later." She was shaking her head and waving her hand, cutting off any further conversation from me. I thought she said that because Barry was still talking and she didn't understand what I was talking about.

We left to go to the restaurant for a bite to eat. As soon as we settled in at home, I quietly said to my wife, "You know, I think I saw a little boy." She got all excited. "No, really. Nah. Really?" Immediately the phone rang. My wife picked it up. It was Patti, who said:

"I saw two little boys peeking out from the opening on the second floor. They were on their hands and knees. I never saw faces. One put his head down and was backing away as soon as I saw him. He had brown hair."

My wife Steph said, "Patti was all charged, the words just tumbled out of her mouth, uncontrolled."

Patti took a deep breath and continued talking to me now.

"I waved my hands at Rob to stop talking because I didn't want him to say anything that might cloud what I saw. This way, what we each saw was validated without influence from the other. When we talked about it later, we both realized that because of Rob's position, standing next to me, he could only see one boy. I saw two boys.

"Even though I knew what I saw, at first...it's just hard to believe. I didn't really believe it until I said it aloud."

This dim view of the opening to the second floor of the schoolhouse shows restoring is needed up there. It also revealed two little boys peeking downstairs — two little boys from more than a century ago. *From the author's collection.*

Patti very excitedly called me later that same night after the Rout to tell me what she saw. Rob's wife emailed me the following day to tell me of Rob's experience.

I returned a few days after the interview to take photos of the schoolhouse. It was a bright, still afternoon. No wind was about — perfect for taking pictures. I left the key in the door and the door open. The entire time I spent there, approximately twenty minutes, the key fob swung back and forth like the pendulum of a clock.

The door stands open letting the sunny day flow into the Clara Barton Schoolroom. The key fob in the lock swung back and forth for twenty minutes when no wind stirred and no vibration occurred. *From the author's collection*.

The Secret Room

A *story presented on the Ghost Walk for several years is the following:*

Quakers first settled early Bordentown when it became known as Farnsworth's Landing, before the Borden family (also Quakers) arrived. They also settled the surrounding countryside. The Quaker Meeting House on Farnsworth Avenue was built in the 1700s. The Borden family donated the land it was built on. It's restored and still in use today by the Bordentown Historical Society.

It's common knowledge that the Quakers were very prominent in aiding fugitive slaves on the Underground Railroad during the early 1800s up through the Civil War. There were three major routes that included New Jersey in its path; two of the paths came into South Jersey, through Bordentown and into the surrounding area, then going north to Princeton, and on to New York. Many of the slaves went even further north, into Canada. The other route traveled up along the Delaware River in eastern Pennsylvania, crossed over to Trenton, and also continued on to New York.

Bordentown was known as Station B East. It was a heavily used and important 'depot' along the way. The surrounding area contained many 'safe' houses too. Many of these old houses once occupied by Quakers in town still have telltale signs of hidden rooms.

The slaves generally traveled at night, going from one 'stop' on the railroad, perhaps ten to twenty miles, waiting for a message that it was safe to move to the next 'stop' on the way. This was a grand effort of many people; some guiding the slaves, some hiding them, and others contributing money, food, or clothing.

This building in the heart of town is nearing two hundred years old. The owner at one time had a chiropractic office on the first floor with an apartment upstairs. Photography was the gentleman's hobby. To utilize space he decided to remodel the basement, installing a darkroom at the far end for developing his photographs. During this remodeling process he uncovered a false ceiling revealing a secret room. There was an area inside hiding the dropped down ceiling that could hold a few runaway slaves if anyone came to the door searching for them. Recovering runaway slaves was a lucrative scheme. High rewards were offered to anyone turning a fugitive slave back to his owner. People giving refuge to runaways could be prosecuted.

Remodeling or restoring a house seems to stir up ghosts and spirits that have been quiet for a long time. It's as if the physical process of moving walls and ceilings reawakens the long-sleeping spirits. Since the remodeling, whenever he came downstairs and through the basement to the rear where his darkroom was located, a coldness hit him. It chilled him right to the bones. It wasn't a draft type of coldness, but he always checked the windows anyway. He never found them open. They were always closed and locked. There were no other openings in the basement that could cause a draft.

Finally, after experiencing this coldness for some time, he called his friend and clairvoyant Adrienne. A 'ghost walk' was conducted. She saw a woman seated in a rocking chair in the area of the secret room. The woman was weeping, holding a baby in her arms. A dead man's body sprawled on the floor. They appeared to be dressed in the clothing style from the mid-1800s.

The secret room indicates that this building was probably a 'safe' house on the Underground Railroad. Other old houses in town were also known as stops on the railroad carrying former slaves to a better life.

The clairvoyant spoke to them softly, encouraging them to go on to the next plane in peace, leaving their pain and suffering behind.

The gentleman was then free to pursue his hobby and go to the darkroom in comfort with no chilling, cold reminders of a time long gone.

Old Ironsides

He's been seen walking along the edge of his property, where the Delaware River slaps against the shore, on many nights when the moon is full. Walking slowly, thoughtfully with his head bent down to meet his hand rising up. Walking alone.

Charles Stewart was born the eighth child of Irish immigrants in Philadelphia in 1776, descended from Scottish and English royal ancestry. His father died while he was still a young lad. Probably because of that he joined a ship as a cabinboy when he was thirteen years old.

In 1798 he chose the American Navy to build his career after the second highest commission as a Lieutenant was offered to him. He commanded his first war ship at twenty-one. At twenty-four he commanded a full brig-o-war, distinguishing himself against Tripoli pirates. At twenty-eight he held the then-highest rank in the U. S. Navy.

As commander of the frigate *USS Constitution*, (nicknamed Old Ironsides) during the War of 1812 Stewart's performance was noted exemplary. He successfully ran the Boston blockade, eluding the British and later capturing a schooner and several smaller vessels. Under his command, the ship sailed for the seas near Madeira where he encountered the British ships *Cyane* and *Levant*. He captured both in a two-against-one fight. Heading home with his prizes, he ran into a British squadron that reclaimed the *Levant*. Stewart still managed to bring the *Cyane* back to the New York port. The War of 1812 ended with Stewart receiving a gold medal from Congress. The crew received considerable prize monies.

Stephan Decatur, a friend from his youth, also built a fine reputation and status in the U.S. Navy. Their third childhood friend, Richard Rush, distinguished himself in the political arena.

His actions at sea were unmatched. He was daring, fierce and successful. He was appointed Commodore, again the highest rank in the American Navy. He served sixty-three years in the American Navy, more than anyone else, ever.

Years earlier the beautiful young Delia Tudor of Boston, Massachusetts' society came into his life. They married in 1803. It was a marriage that produced two children, Charles and Delia, and near disaster for the Commodore.

The command of the entire Pacific on the *USS Franklin* was his from 1820 to 1824. During this time in the Pacific, his wife and children were aboard ship when disaster struck. Delia secretly smuggled a spy named Madrid on board the ship without her husband's knowledge. An international crisis arose. Commander Stewart was brought up on charges to a court martial. This was a staggering event that nearly marred his brilliant naval career. Stewart was absolved of all charges when Delia's actions were revealed. He sought a divorce.

He moved to Bordentown, New Jersey to his two hundred twenty-five acre estate purchased from Francois Frederici in 1816—a mansion that the General of Suriname built in 1797. The property sat on a high bluff, bordering and overlooking the Delaware River. He named it Montpellier, but everyone else affectionately called it "Old Ironsides."

He next became Naval Commissioner from 1830 to 1832. Then, he moved on to become Commander of the Philadelphia Naval Yard.

He was appointed to the office of the first Commander of the Home Guard. A candidacy for President of the United States was offered, but he never desired it. His personal life was considered unstable. His divorce situation was a mark of shame in that day's society.

Before he retired from the Navy in 1861, he wrote recommendations and guidelines that were followed in forming a modern navy and in creating a naval school. Congress promoted him to the newly established rank of Rear Admiral (retired). In 1864, he was the only surviving officer of either civil or military service of the USA who held a commission granted in the eighteenth century. He was a man who met President George Washington, was recognized by President Thomas Jefferson, advised President James Madison, and was consulted by President Abraham Lincoln. He was a friend of the former King of Spain, Joseph Bonaparte, and maintained friendly correspondence with Emperor Napoleon III. The man's career record was brilliant.

His nickname was Old Ironsides. He was obviously a man of passion, daring and adventure. He sailed all over the world, but chose Bordentown as his homeport. Here he was recognized as being a quiet country gentleman living on his estate with his mistress, Margaret, with whom he had three children, Charlotte, Julia, and Edward. Here his love of children, flowers, birds, and his farm was common knowledge. Here his daughter and granddaughter, Delia Stewart Parnell and Fanny Parnell (respectively mother and sister of Charles Stewart Parnell, leader of Irish Home Rule in Ireland), also chose as their home. Here also, Fanny Parnell later became internationally known for her work with the Irish Land League. Here the famous came to visit and seek advice from the famous Fanny Parnell herself.

Here, where he found peace from his battles, Rear Admiral Charles Stewart is seen from time to time in the dark of the evening. Walking along the edge of his property, where his land and the Delaware River slap together like his professional and his private life. Walking under the full moon. Walking alone.

Old Stone Shanty
(as it relates to Old Ironsides)

Juriaan Francois Frederici built a mansion high on a bluff overlooking the Delaware River in 1797. He was then Governor-General of the South American Dutch Colony, Suriname. At his command an old stone shanty was added to the property on the down slope to the river.

Frederici, born in 1751, first went to Paramaribo, Suriname in 1762 to become a cadet in the militia. As he grew, his strength in fighting runaway slaves brought from Africa promoted him to lieutenant, then captain.

His career continued to escalate as captain, leading European soldiers and the Black Rangers of Suriname. The Black Rangers had taken an oath not to kill any Africans or descendents regardless of the situation. But when the Boni-Maroons (escaped African slaves) rose up against the European planters during the first Boni-Maroon War, the Black Rangers in one regiment forgot their oath. Eleven were captured; one was shot; one slave was tortured after the gun pointed at him misfired twice, then they sent him back to the colonists; and nine were killed by machete.

Suriname was the most brutal of all the slave countries. Violence and terror were used in an attempt to control the slaves. Sadistic beatings were common, sometimes resulting in death. When enslavers caught a runaway slave, they cut his Achilles tendon. A second runaway offense resulted in the slave's right leg being amputated. Plantations were being raided by the Maroons to free the slaves. They were carrying off as many slaves as possible, then inviting them to fight the Colonists. They created their own communities to the west and south of Suriname, in the jungles of this South American country. A few managed to eventually sign peace treaties with the Netherlands.

Captain Frederici successfully raided the Maroon stronghold camp of Buku, capturing and killing the runaway slaves. For his actions he was promoted to colonel.

In 1792 he was elevated to Governor-General. He retained that position when the English took over the colony. When the Dutch again took control of the colony in 1802, they suspended him. Reasons were not forthcoming.

By then Frederici was operating a plantation in Suriname and had built a mansion and working farm in Bordentown. He died in Suriname in 1812. Commodore Charles Stewart bought his farm and mansion in 1816.

A Mr. Block owned the Old Stone Shanty after Frederici passed, using it for an icehouse. He sold it to Fred Gilmore, who sold it to Commodore Charles Stewart. In 1830 the Shanty was used as a washhouse for washing clothes since buildings were few and laborers building the Camden & Amboy Railroad were many. The Shanty just stood there, deserted, after the railroad was completed.

But the haunting of the Old Stone Shanty goes back to Frederici, a man commonly known in Bordentown for his hot temper and violent ways. A man accustomed to the sadistic treatment of slaves in Suriname...He was a man who built his military and political career by brutally breaking the backs of runaway African slaves trying to live in peace.

He was reputed to have beaten a bound servant to death in the Old Stone Shanty. The ghost of the poor unfortunate man is known to wander this most desolate area between Bordentown City and White Hill after daylight hours ended. Before the dawn comes, moans and screams could be heard from the Old Stone Shanty by tramps and hoboes that found a spot near the railroad to settle in for the night. The shanty became notorious for housing smugglers and murderers. But none of them stayed there after dark.

Finally, by 1877, the crumbling stones were removed. Fresh young grass was planted to create a park-like effect, creating a resting place for a poor soul beaten to death by his master.

The Udell Affair: Gerry's Story...

My Aunt Ople Rockwell owned this building on Farnsworth Avenue way back in the 1940s when she opened the Charm Beauty Shop here. She did hairstyling, cosmetology, and coloring. My Aunt May Lundeen worked for her along with a few other women. In those days Marion Aaronson and Marion Stewart were around town. Aunt Ople was in the Chamber of Commerce. She was very active in the town and knew everybody.

I moved into the upstairs apartment around 1955. My cousin Joan lived part of the time above the shop and part down the Jersey shore, too.

Unlike most beauty salons, Aunt Ople wasn't open on Saturdays. She owned a house down the shore at Harvey Cedars and was determined to spend weekends there. Her shop was open on Thursday and Friday nights to make up for being closed on Saturdays.

My field was accounting then. I did all the business books for Aunt Ople. On Thursday nights I came into the shop late to do the payroll. Fridays were pay day for her employees. Most of the time I was alone because they all went out to eat on Thursdays after the shop closed around ten o'clock, sometimes later.

Not long after I began at Aunt Ople's on a particular late Thursday night I was alone in the building. Joan must have been out on a date. I was sitting inside the front door at the desk in the quiet, working on the books, when I heard a click. My head bobbed up and my ears perked up. My senses were at high tide. I knew that sound. Chills dashed up my spine. I was alone.

It was the latch on the door to the basement, just beyond the shop. And I was alone. I listened intently. No other sounds were made. No footsteps, no movement meaning someone was there. No squeaky floorboards. Nothing. After a deep breath, I went back to the books. Relief washed over me when I heard the ladies returning from dinner.

Soon I learned that the click of the cellar door happened often. The handle came up with a click and the cellar door would open. Once I understood that it was a common occurrence and harmless, I'd just go back and push the latch down again, hard. Then I would head up front to go back to work, hurrying now to do the figures, and darn if I wouldn't hear it again! Click. Some folks said, "You're crazy, it's your imagination."

Over and over I said, "I am not. I know what I hear and see with that door."

"Finally," I said to myself, "I'm gonna find out what's causing that."

So I went through the open door, heading down the steps and glanced up. Ack! I saw something hanging from the rafters. I beat it back upstairs and slammed the door shut! Later I found out they were Uncle Ed's fishing waders. Hanging there, they looked like a dead body flopped over.

After the waders episode, I never felt afraid. I never felt any cold air spots and I never saw anything. But I know about that door. Something clicked that latch and opened that door. It appeared to me to be an innocent happening.

I eventually changed careers and got my real estate license in 1968 and my aunt's building was my first listing for sale. I sold it to Ralph and Joyce.

Around the late 1990s the Ghost Walk began in Bordentown and I finally heard the story behind the click. It went like this:

During the Revolutionary War years, a group of promi-nent men decided to construct floating mines such as they heard were being used in the New York Harbor. Colonel Joseph Borden, Colonel Oakey Hoagland, Colonel Kirk-bride, and Caleb Carman called upon four town mechanics for their assistance. The mechanics, Joseph Plowman, a pin maker who created a design for spring locks to use as firing mechanisms, the Bunting Brothers who were both blacksmiths, and Robert Jackaway, the gun shopkeeper, made the floating mines.

The idea was to float these 'marine turtles' down the river to the British ships anchored in the Philadelphia Harbor expecting them to blow up the ships upon contact. But that night the British pulled their ships close into the harbor because the river was heavy with floating chunks of ice. Seeing the 'floating turtles' blow up the chunks of ice they came in contact with spooked the Brits enough to shoot at everything that moved in the water. They became the joke of the day, and this action became known as the "Battle of the Kegs."

In retaliation for this act of rebellion, and to restore fear and respect, the British headed up the Delaware River. They docked in the harbor at Bordentown. The next day at noon, they unloaded cannon and marched up Main Street. Then they opened fire.

During this time period, Mrs. Idell lived on Main Street south of Walnut. It was her habit every day to sit in the doorway and watch the events going on in town. She rocked back and forth in her rocking chair gossiping with the folks traversing up and down the street.

When the British fired that cannon, a ball struck the building behind her and ricocheted, hitting the back of her rocking chair. The cannon ball never touched her, but the shock of the situation sent her to bed.

During the time spent in Bordentown by the British, the soldiers broke into homes and businesses, helped themselves to liquor and food. Windows were smashed, and other destruction to the property of the residents followed. One of four local young men coming into town to see what was going on, Edward Idell, the son of Mrs. Idell, was captured at the foot of Walnut Street and brutally murdered on the spot. The shock and heartbreak was too much for Mrs. Idell. She died three days later.

Past owners of this building always had difficulty keeping the entrance door to the basement closed. No matter how tightly the door was secured, it would pop open again and again. Even when the door was locked it would be found open a short time later.

Finally, a psychic friend suggested turning the door, placing the hinges on the opposite side. The door has since remained shut after it's been latched.

It's believed that the spirit of Mrs. Idell, coming out of the cellar, was bound to this location by the strong emotion of love for her only son killed so early in his lifetime.

Bellevue

*T*his story has been told on the Ghost Walk held each October in Bordentown. Parts of the story come directly from a letter in the Horvath-Strunk Collection.

Colonel Joseph Kirkbride was the third generation of Kirkbrides in the colonies. His grandfather Joseph ran away from his master and ran to the New World in 1681. He found employment in Pennsbury Manor, opposite Bordentown. His first wife, Phoebe, lived only a few years. His second wife was the daughter of Mahlon and Rebeckah Stacy, founders of Trenton, New Jersey. He began with next to nothing and from that he built an influential and wealthy estate, eventually owning Bellevue in Pennsbury Manor. In 1699 he returned to England where he repaid his old master for the services denied him years earlier before returning once again to the colonies.

Joseph Kirkbride II died in 1748 when our Colonel was seventeen years old, leaving him to manage the vast estate and Kirkbride Ferry Service that crossed between Penn's Manor and Bordentown. Trade across the Delaware River was common and he built esteem on the Jersey side to match his reputation on the Pennsylvania side of the river.

The Colonel became a representative to the Legislature of Pennsylvania and a member of the first General Convention of the State. This is about the time he became acquainted with Thomas Paine, secretary to the Convention and later author of *Common Sense* and *The Rights of Man*. Both men were devoted Patriots, and they formed a life-long friendship.

Early in the Revolutionary War, Joseph, then a lieutenant, gathered recruits, arms, ammunition and other supplies needed for the fighting men. He also housed and quartered many recruits and militia on his estate and that of his cousin Jonathan's. Soon he was promoted to the rank of Colonel.

The British sailed up the Delaware River to punish Bordentown's people in retaliation for the floating mines sent downriver to blow up the British ships anchored in the Philadelphia harbor. They burned Colonel Borden's house, ravaged the town, breaking windows and furniture, and pillaged what they could carry. When they finished with Bordentown, they crossed the river, sought out the Colonel's Bellevue Plantation and burned everything on it.

Before the smoke of the Revolutionary War even dissolved, before the Brits and Hessians went home (actually some of them stayed), the Colonel bought land at the Hilltop from longtime friend Colonel Borden. They were also loosely connected by marriage, as Captain Joseph Borden (Colonel Borden's son) married Colonel Kirkbride's niece. Bordentown became his permanent residence in 1780.

There on the Hilltop he built a new Bellevue for his bride, Mary Rogers of Allentown, New Jersey. Her brother, Samuel, married Col. Kirkbride's sister, Mary.

The Colonel resumed his habit of inviting friends, distinguished gentlemen of state, and veterans to come and stay at his large estate. Thomas Paine remained a close friend and considered Bellevue home, staying with his old friend whenever he was in Bordentown. The Colonel entertained, generously extending a welcome to many, and especially lavishly on holidays when guests were always in attendance. Visitors would often come and stay for a month or two at a time.

His cousin Helen Secord and her six-year-old daughter were residing with the Kirkbrides during December and the Christmas holiday season of 1791. She was the wife of Captain Secord, a man who spent more time on the sea than on land. Presently he was on a three-year voyage going around Cape Horn to India.

Theirs was an arranged marriage. Before her parents introduced them, Helen was joyously in love with Richard Havilland. They were betrothed and she was looking forward to a life of promise and happiness. But that didn't last long. Under pressure and insistence from her parents, she broke her engagement to Richard and married the man they chose for her, the wealthy Captain Secord.

The Captain brought his wife, a lovely, graceful, and accomplished woman, to his homeport of Philadelphia to live after the birth of their daughter.

Colonel Kirkbride invited Helen and her daughter to be his guests for the holiday season in his Bordentown Estate because he was concerned that she was without family for the holidays in Philadelphia. She was proficient in music and performed skillfully, surely an asset to any holiday party. Unusual for her, she presently exuded a quiet, thoughtfulness about her.

Unknown to others, Mrs. Secord and Richard Havilland began to spend time together again. Mr. Haviland was always a frequent visitor to the Kirkbride mansion. He, too, was an expected guest this Christmas Eve. They also concealed from everyone that Richard had been pressing Helen to run off with him.

He wrote to her. "Life has been intolerable without you, Helen. Nothing is as it should be, when you are not with me." Richard implored. "For you to live alone while your husband is out to sea is also no way to live your life."

They made plans for Helen to quietly slip away from the mansion under cover of night and meet Richard on Chapel Lane (now West Church Street). His friend, David Carter, made arrangements for them to travel to New York. There they planned to board ship and sail on to Paris where their unmarried status would be accepted.

As usual the established Kirkbride Christmas traditions at Bellevue were set. On Christmas Eve, personal friends and families were invited for an elaborate soiree. On Christmas morning, the Colonel opened his doors to the Bordentown community. The tables were again laden with food and liquid refreshments for them to enjoy. Colonel Kirkbride was never present on Christmas morning, but the servants carried out his instructions to also admit the drummers and fifes for the entertainment of the townsfolk.

Finally, it was Christmas Eve! A snowstorm began falling softly in the early afternoon. As evening neared, the earth was covered with a white blanket of snow. Candles gleamed from every window. The season was at hand.

All was astir! A large party assembled in compliance with the Colonel's wishes to partake of some cheer. Music was proposed. Mrs. Secord was asked to perform. She took her position by the instrument and, with a clear voice, played and sang a ballad. After singing for a time, she quietly withdrew, passed down the hall, and entered one of the rooms. Her little daughter followed her into the room. The mother selected and donned some warm clothing from the wardrobe. Then she took her little daughter into her arms, kissed, and embraced her.

"Where are you going, Mama?" "I am going out, darling. You tell Uncle Joseph that I leave you in his care. Be a good little girl for him." She made a brief visit to the library, retraced her steps, and passed out of the door at the rear of the house.

The little girl returned to the circle of guests after her mother's departure. Finding herself the subject of attention, she forgot her mother's instructions. Her mother left the house at nine o'clock. Nearly an hour passed when someone remarked of the whereabouts of Mrs. Secord. The child then tugged at Colonel Kirkbride's arm to give him her mother's message. The night was cold and the snow was still falling lightly. The Colonel could not imagine where Mrs. Secord had gone and decided to wait an hour before announcing her departure so as to not alarm his other guests.

He returned to his party. The old clock in the hall rounded the hour of eleven. Now he had to do something. The Colonel spoke softly to three of his guests and the four of them retired to the library to decide on a next step. The silence could be kept no longer. Word spread throughout the village. Search parties were organized. Torches lit up the landscape. Nothing was found but some footprints — from the rear door down to the rivers edge. A quantity of snow had fallen. In some areas the foot tracks were faint, but definitely a woman's and they terminated at the edge of the river.

The following day was sorrowful. Colonel Kirkbride went to his library desk and found a letter under his paperweight.

"My Dear Kinsman ... If I have sinned much, I have sorrowed much. I have no excuse for the step I am about to take. Even if I gave one, it would not palliate in your mind, the course I am to pursue. To the last I shall retain for you, feelings of gratitude. I leave this house this night beset with alternatives. The one—to unite my destiny with the person to whom I first plighted my vows and should have married; the other—to end all conflicting earthly emotions and in a sense cover my sins beneath the cold waters of the river. By the time you read this note, one of these will have been chosen."

The following May some fishermen found a woman's body near the mouth of Crosswicks and Barge Creek. According to the dress still on the body, it was identified as Helen Secord.

Some twenty years later, Mr. Havilland learned of the fate of his beloved Helen through some old friends from the colonies that he met in Paris. At the time he thought Helen decided not to leave her husband. A broken-hearted Richard left for Paris and remained there. Now he returned to Bordentown, inquired of Mrs. Secord's burial, and left a bouquet of red roses on her grave.

Many, many years have passed, but from time to time it is reported that a lady in a flowing dress is seen gliding across the lawn from where the former cherished home of the Colonel Kirkbride mansion Bellevue once stood, down to the river's edge.

Burr's Corner

*A*nother story told in recent years on the annual Bordentown Ghost Walk is that of Samuel Engle Burr Jr.

At one time the southeast corner at Farnsworth Avenue and Crosswicks Street housed Samuel E. Burr's (Sr.) General Store and home. He arrived in Bordentown in 1859 from Moorestown, New Jersey. His businesses occupied space on Farnsworth Avenue for many years. He also held political offices in Bordentown and did some undercover work for the Union during the Civil War. He was a cousin to the Confederate's First Lady, Varina Howell (Mrs. Jefferson) Davis. His reputation and integrity were spotless. Sam and his second wife, Elizabeth Thompson Burr, raised their two children, Samuel Engle Jr. and Anna, at this location.

Early in the 1900s Sam Jr. played with a little boy in white. He was a child no one saw except young Sam. In later years he explained that the boy was a figment of his imagination, but he could describe the boy and remember that they only played when they were alone. Never when other children or adults were around. The boy always wore a white suit and was willing to do anything Sam wanted to do. His mother accepted the little boy in white because she possessed a developed psychic ability herself. His father felt strongly that Sam should not be conjuring up shadows and playing with them.

That's exactly how people lose the psychic ability that comes naturally to a child. Adults ridicule it out of them until it disappears.

His mother saw things from time to time. Once, it was a pick and shovel in the upstairs hallway. She announced that it indicated a coming death. Her husband pooh-poohed the whole idea because he passed the hallway several times that morning and had seen nothing. Her cousin Mattie passed over on the following day. No one else saw the pick and shovel and it was not their habit to keep those tools in the upstairs hallway.

The whole idea completely exasperated her husband.

Sam's mother told him several times about a spirit being in the house. Once, while she was rocking and quietly sewing some napkins, Sam Jr. was laying on the floor drawing pictures in a book. She told him she was going upstairs because someone wanted to tell her something. *She apparently confided those moments to her son because he understood and her husband did not. It's hard to get some people to believe until it happens to them. That works all the time.*

One day during a severe thunderstorm she went upstairs because she felt someone was up there. When she arrived, she saw a man going through her bureau. When she appeared he began jumping up and down waving his arms. Then he ran away. She called her husband. He could find nothing and blamed her imagination.

Sam's mother also believed in dream interpretation. Again, her husband furiously disapproved, calling it a heathen practice and very un-Christian. Elizabeth didn't agree. She hid her multiple dream books between the linens along with her planchette board. She used the planchette board only occasionally. It never became a habit.

Sam's younger sister, Miss Anna T. Burr, declares she knows nothing of her family's psychic abilities. She was associated for thirty-four years with the Bordentown Education System. First, she was a teacher for ten years and then an administrator. She's written histories, biographies and genealogies of Bordentown. At this writing in 2007, she has recently celebrated her 107th birthday and is still getting around under her own power. The Burr name is familiar yet today, to anyone who has truly lived in Bordentown City.

Part Three:

Township Sightings

R estaurants and businesses now line the two State Highways 130 and 206 (they cross like an "X") in Bordentown Township. The Bordentown Cemetery have tombstones dating from 1810 and continue to expand. But until Bossert Builders began constructing the Bossert Estates in the 1950s, the township remained mostly farmland.

The farmers who settled here in the late 1600s and early 1700s (mostly Quakers) built homes along Crosswicks Creek. Prior to that the Unami tribe of the Lenni-Lenape Native Americans utilized the area for hunting, growing their vegetables, and trading with other tribes. The land was used for great meetings. The Quakers who came into the area first treated the Natives with respect and honesty. That changed as the countryside became populated.

More Than One Ghost:
Nancy's Story...

We bought our house in the 1970s. The man we bought the house from owned it since the mid-1940s. He had lived here with his parents, raised his children here, and got old here. He loved the house. When we sat at the settlement table, I could see the tears well up in his eyes at letting the house go. I got a little teary myself when I looked up at his face. Less than a year after we bought the house, he passed away.

We were very happy to move into the house. It's the only house I've ever owned and I've only lived in two others, my mother's house and my grandmother's for awhile. Always old houses. I've always lived surrounded with things that once belonged to other people. I've always lived with the spirits and memories of people.

Someone once complimented me on a handkerchief tucked into my vest pocket. I replied, "Oh, that's the handkerchief Rose gave me when we cleaned out her mother's house." The woman gasped and answered me, "You're wearing the hanky of a dead person!"

I smiled. Everything I own is old — it's a heirloom to me. They're treasures. I have no problem with that. I guess that's why I've always been open to spirits. I once saw a ghost in my grandmother's house on Park Street. Her house is gone now.

My daughters were riding bicycles with training wheels when I looked through the front storm door to check on them. I saw a stooped-looking older man, short jacket, and soft cap carrying a lunch kettle coming in the gate. I opened the storm door and he was gone. Poof! I'm certain it was my father's Uncle Andy. He may have stood in that same spot long ago and watched me learning to ride a bike.

My daughter has seen both of my parents here in this house. When I went to tell her my mother died, she said, "I know." I suspect Mom stopped to see her in passing over.

My parents loved this house. They helped us move in, they helped us fix it up, they were very proud of us. They knew the house. I can see them being here by choice.

When my oldest granddaughter was just an infant, a fortune teller in a restaurant was entranced with her. She picked her up and carried her all around the room. When she returned her, she told my daughter, "She's a very old soul." A seer knows.

We started hearing noises shortly after we moved into the house. There were no shutters on this house when we moved in. They were burned during the depression for fuel, so we didn't hear a banging shutter. We heard someone walking across the wooden floors downstairs when we were upstairs. When we were downstairs, she seemed to be upstairs. There were no rugs at the time, so it was very clear. We dubbed her the high-heeled lady and laughed. We didn't hear her all the time or at any special time. We don't hear her for years at a time, and then suddenly, she'll be back, often when we have overnight guests.

At one point I was standing in my kitchen and I looked through the doorway and saw what I thought was the man we bought the house from pulling up his pants over long johns. Well, how can I be afraid of a ghost pulling up his pants? And that had been his bedroom. To myself I thought, "I guess he's back."

Years went by, the kids grew up, and life goes on. My daughter became engaged to marry. Her fiancée's new jeep was parked outside the dining room bay windows. I was cutting fabric on the dining room table when I looked out to see a young man, blond-haired, admiring the jeep.

My son-in-law has lots of cousins, most of them tall and blond.

I went to the door to introduce myself. No one was there. I looked around; no one was anywhere. Then I realized that although all the windows were open I had not heard a car come up the drive. With this long dirt and stone driveway, I always hear when a car pulls in. And this house is out in the country. It's unlikely anyone is going to walk here.

A few years passed. For some unknown reason, when Easter came, I decided to go to church. I didn't go very often and have no idea why I went that particular day. In church my cousin's son, who also rarely goes to church, sat next to me.

We started shooting the breeze and he said to me, "Hey, I met someone who used to live in your house. I took a class and met this guy. He was there in the summertime during the Depression. The guy didn't really live there; he came with his mother to visit the people living there for a couple weeks. He described the house and mentioned there was no furniture except in the kitchen and bedroom. The couple's three-year-old boy was a neat little kid. As an afterthought he murmured that the boy was killed in his teens."

So we're sitting in church and I'm thinking. "Teenage farm boy. Tractor. If you were a teenage boy and you saw this neat new jeep sitting in the driveway, wouldn't you like to check it out? Hmm... Sounds about right to me."

"Frank, ask him if the boy was blonde-haired." He did. And he was. "Think 'Sound of Music.' He said, the family was German." (Sic)

At my cousin's request, the older man sent me a letter describing his summer on the Bordentown farm. He wrote: "There was no indoor plumbing or electricity in the house during the 1930s. I remember skimming the cream off the milk and making butter in a churn. They had a chicken coop out back with lots of chickens. They used a hand pump in a shallow well in the back for all drinking, bathing and water for the farm animals. The outhouse lighting was a kerosene lantern."

He wrote that they plowed with horses. The backfields were for wheat and corn for the horses, cows, and chickens. They grew sweet corn, tomatoes, carrots, asparagus, strawberries, pumpkins and peanuts in the side field to sell at the market in Trenton. The lady had an old Ford truck fitted out like a market stand.

He continued to write about the way times were in those days: Milk and bread were delivered to the door then. The iceman brought blocks of ice every couple of days. Men with pushcarts sold bananas and fresh ground horseradish. Ice cream cones were two dips for a nickel.

I researched the newspaper and found an article about the accident. It stated that the nineteen-year-old burned to death when a rotary hay-baling machine he was making adjustments on caught fire, setting the load of hay ablaze. He neglected to turn the motor off when the machine jammed. His arm caught in the machine's mechanism. In a matter of seconds he was gone. He was an only child.

The newspaper article said that he was a graduate of William MacFarland High School. I just happened to have a copy of the yearbook for his graduation year (no ghost here — it belonged to my brother). I looked into the smiling face of a young man who must have been looking forward to a long and interesting life. A life full of fun and friends and new cars.

I asked my neighbor, the son of the man I bought the house from, about the story.

"Yes, it's true. We weren't here yet, but I heard the story, too."

"By the way, I've seen your father in my house, too."

"I'm not surprised," he told me. "My father loved that house. If he's anywhere, he's there. It was my father, my grandfather and me that restored the house to its' present condition."

For parting thoughts, Nancy commented:

"**Synchronicity is definitely at work here. Starting with my not usually going to church, to meet my cousin, who rarely goes to church, and we're talking about his meeting someone who has stayed in my house and could fill in some details for us. I think our young man wants it known that he lived here. We don't mind sharing the house with spirits since it's obvious that they were happy here and that they love the house as much as we do.**"

The Wounded Ghost?
Helene's Story...

Tom and I were newlyweds when we rented the second floor apartment, including a full walk-up attic in an old farmhouse on Crosswicks Road. This was in 1966, after Charles Bossert built the first two sections of Bossert Estates, but the third section wasn't completed yet. The area was farmland and not much else. When we looked out the windows at night we saw darkness. No street lights, no traffic lights, no cars driving up and down the street either. It was a dark, quiet area.

Our apartment was laid out in a square with the steps coming up in the middle. It contained a kitchen, nook, dining room, living room, and bedroom. A bath, of course. When I was in one room, I could see into all the other rooms. The cross-breeze was wonderful with the windows open on all sides. The walk-up attic was complete with a floor and finished walls. We didn't use that at all. It remained empty.

We both worked days, Tom enrolled in classes at night. While he was gone I would straighten up the rooms, wondering why Tom moved things from where I placed them on the coffee table onto the end tables. I didn't expect him to even notice the little knick-knacks and vases. I thought it strange for him to move them around. Oh, well, I didn't say anything. It was a small thing to fuss over.

I kept the salt and pepper shakers in a certain place on the kitchen table. Often I found them moved to a different area. You know when there are only two of you living in an apartment and one of you is gone a lot of the time, well, it kinda makes you wonder. But it was another small thing, so I let it go.

If I went to bed early to read before Tom came home, I'd hear a 'walk, drag, walk, drag' coming from the attic and think I have to ask Tom what kind of an animal would make that sound. I'm a city girl and can't identify country animal noises. I forgot about it. Time went on. I still heard that distinctive sound now and again, just never mentioned it to Tom.

Summer came and lots of violent thunderstorms came with it. One night we lay in bed, asleep, when I was jolted awake by lightning. Great rumbles of thunder roared and lightning cracked, shattering the quiet of the countryside. All the windows lit up around the apartment. It seemed the light was coming from all directions. My eyes were wide open watching the lightning. Just as suddenly as the lightning struck again, a movement suddenly caught my eye across the apartment. It was a dark shadow in a formal military uniform. My eyes were bulging by now. I screamed. It disappeared.

I never saw him again after that. Things were still moved around from one place to another.

As the fall approached we decided to paint the rooms to take the dinginess away from the old house. We were sprucing it up for the holidays. I placed the cans of paint in the rooms I chose to paint a particular color. Before long I found the cans moved from one room to another. Now I knew it wasn't Tom. He would never do that.

I still heard footsteps and a drag in the attic. Now I knew it wasn't an animal. I wondered if the resident who shared our apartment had been wounded. If so, in which war.

Part Four:

Area Hauntings

The Unsettled House In Cranbury: Jean's Story...

My husband and I were looking for a home in central Jersey. We were moving from the New Brunswick area because our house had become very small after our third child was born. We started looking in Cranbury, a quaint little town with a country feeling to it. It was first settled, other than the Lenape tribe of the Delaware Indians, in 1680. The town became a stagecoach stop for travelers crossing from New York City to Philadelphia.

One day I met with the realtor who knew I liked older houses. My husband preferred something more modern. When she began to describe the house, I immediately knew which one she meant. It was an old Victorian set on an incline away from the center of town by maybe three or four blocks. I just felt I was destined to live in that house.

I drove to Cranbury and, sure enough, it was the house I'd been dreaming about.

We walked through the house while I was carrying my toddler. I saw out the back that a swimming pool was set in the field without a fence around it. Must put a fence around that right away, I thought to myself. Not safe.

The house was beautiful, but needed some work; a second floor roof leak was dripping into a bucket. It had plenty of room. Each of my three children could have their own room. So many possibilities. The owner walked us through the house. She had very sad eyes. I thought to myself, I wonder what her story is; she's lovely and gracious, but looks so sad.

I asked the Realtor about the woman and she filled me in. "She's going through an unhappy divorce. They have four children, ages ranging from 10 to 16." Horrible, I thought. I left a $100 deposit.

The next day I toured a private school I wanted for my middle child, our older daughter, to attend. I planned on sending her to high school there. Transport was available. Perfect. Things were going along smoothly. Coincidently our young guide on the tour was also from Cranbury. With my encouragement, she filled me in with information about the family living in my dream house.

"I know the house you're buying. I babysit for those kids. You know, the house has a ghost." She went on after my prodding her. "A long time ago a little girl drowned in the well."

When I heard that statement. I froze. Now everything changed. A steel door shut in my brain. It just closed any desire I held for that house. I no longer wanted it. Now there was something very foreboding about that household.

"They have a lot of occurrences — doors slamming, things falling off shelves, things breaking, noises, unexplained furniture being moved, items moved with no explanation. They brought in experts to make peace with the ghost so the family could live in comfort."

I was totally engrossed. She continued. "Yes, they changed doorways, put in windows and made other minor changes." While she was talking I remembered seeing a beautiful white organza Victorian dress, freshly washed and starched, just hanging in the earthen basement without a bag over it. It seemed so strange.

"I know what you mean," the girl said picking up on my thoughts. "They hang it there to make peace with the ghost."

I told my husband about our conversation and explained to him how I felt. He tried to talk me out of it, calling my stance silly. He hadn't seen the house, so the next day I went back to the house with him and the realtor. I noticed the day was very gray and windy as I was walking from the car to the house. There was not a good feeling, but an eerie presence, around this house. I just wasn't comfortable. My husband tried again to explain everything away. I kept remembering the sadness on the face of the woman who lived there. It just wasn't a happy house. It felt as though something was unfinished there. Something was unsettled in the house. I could feel it. I didn't want to be there. We asked for and received our deposit back.

I later heard the house sold in a tax sale. The family moved away and divorced. It was just so sad. Maybe someday the right family will move in and have what the house and the resident ghost needs to turn the house back into a happy one.

Jean now lives in Bordentown City.

Ghostly Remnants in Hightstown: Rob's Story...

When my wife and I bought an old house in Hightstown, the first thing we did was begin restoration and improvements. One night, exhausted from working in the house, I laid down on my back in bed. I never sleep on my back. I just don't.

In the middle of the night, actually 3 a.m., I felt someone shaking my thigh. My eyes opened, I looked over at Steph. She was sound asleep. I looked the other way and saw a woman wearing a purple gown. It appeared to be velvet and of an earlier period. She was kind of transparent. Her hair was shoulder length and black as night.

As I was about to say 'can I help you?', she began to disappear...from the inside out so there was just a black silhouette of her before she completely dissolved. I woke up Steph, saying, "I think I just saw a ghost."

The next morning when we looked at our comforter, tan in color, we saw little purple threads lying on top. There was nothing in our bedroom that could account for purple threads. Nothing. We saved the bits of threads we found. We still have them.

Rob and his wife now live in Bordentown.

Part Five:

Rumors

The Old Opera House

An old Opera House in town burned and now has apartments in it. We'll call the resident "J." She has a resident ghost, Walter, named after the man who was murdered outside the Opera House many lifetimes ago. He used to play with J's cat. She watched the cat pawing at the air as if there were a string hanging there, but there wasn't one to be seen...not by J anyway. The cat often was playing and jumping as if someone were there with her, but no one could be seen.

After J moved into the apartment she learned quickly not to place anything on the fireplace mantel. The items would disappear! One time J left her wallet and keys on the mantel. What a mess! J ran around the apartment yelling, "It's not funny Walter! Give me back my stuff!" He didn't...at least not right then.

She had new keys made and replaced her license, social security card, ID, credit cards, etc. It was a hard lesson to learn. Some time later, while she was cleaning out her closet, she picked up a pair of old boots. She intended to throw them out. But wait. One felt heavier than the other. Yep. When she turned it upside down, her keys and wallet fell out. J got her things back. Walter got another tongue-lashing.

Waretown Mennonites

Many years ago my sister bought an old church in Waretown and converted it into a house. I loved going down for a visit, but when it came to sleeping there, that was an adventure. I'd wake up from a sound sleep in the middle of the night and see these Mennonites dressed in somber clothing standing at the foot of the bed. They'd stand right there and sternly look at you, fully dressed in pilgrim-like clothes.

A few other people who had also stayed there told my sister they experienced it too.

Lenni Lenape Indians

More than one person has told me stories of seeing Indians in the Bordentown City and Township area. They seem to be spotted more often at night when the moon is full and especially in the autumn. They've been seen just sitting and appearing to be watching. Just watching....

Evidence has been found that the Paleo-Native Americans were in the Bordentown area of New Jersey for 8,000 years prior to the Colonial period. During Colonial times, the Lenni Lenape (pronounced Len-NAH-pay) of the Algonquin Native Americans occupied the area. The Lenape was made up of three tribes; the Unami, with a turtle as totem, settled in central Jersey, the Munsi, with a wolf as totem, in the north, and Unalactigo, with the turkey as totem, in south Jersey. The early European settlers dubbed them the Delawares, identifying the tribe by the Delaware River where they lived.

The tribes were divided into clans. The clans traced their lineage through the females and the females were considered 'head of the household.' Braves were not allowed to marry into their own clans, but needed to go to another clan to find a wife. The Delawares were a peaceful tribe and this custom probably created bonds between the clans, discouraging war among their own tribes.

Together the men hunted, fished and clammed in season. The women also worked communally in farming, gathering, cooking, making clothes, and childcare. But it was in fall of the year when a great number of Native Americans gathered their tribes together in the Bordentown area. They conducted spiritual and religious ceremonies, socialized, renewed family bonds with other clans, and celebrated the success of the hunt and the reaping of foods.

Still today, in the spirit world anyway, the clans can be seen gathering in Bordentown. Sometimes they even get caught on film.

The Jersey Devil

T he legend begins in the Pine Barrens of New Jersey ca. 1735. Mrs. Leeds, suspected of being a witch because of the herbs she grew and the healing she worked, cursed her thirteenth child because she was having a very difficult birth. "The Devil can take this one." She was reported saying. They were a family struggling to survive and she was exhausted. It's said that the baby born was a monster with a grotesque appearance of reptilian body, bat wings and long tail.

Since that day, whenever children, dogs, cats or small livestock animals disappeared, the Jersey Devil was blamed. The bones of the animals were found; children were not. They were gone forever, never to be seen again. Terrified residents asked a local minister to do an exorcism that would last one hundred years. However, one day in the early 1800s American War hero Commodore Stephen Decatur came to the Pine Barrens to test the cannonballs at the Hanover Iron Works. While on the firing range, he noticed a strange creature flying overhead. He aimed and fired at the monster. Witnesses say his shot struck and went right through it. The Devil continued on its way.

The Jersey Devil was reported seen in Bordentown, New Jersey.

Joseph Bonaparte, former King of Spain and brother of Napoleon, was quite used to having the finest of amenities surrounding him on his estate at Pointe Breeze. When he made Bordentown his home in 1817 he brought fine arts, statuary, jewels, and craftsmen from Europe. He personally imported and planted trees, creating a park-like setting on his thousand acre-plus-property for himself, his family and guests to enjoy driving through. Many honorable and noted guests were invited to his estate for the twenty years he lived there including John Quincy Adams, Marquis de Lafayette, Daniel Webster, Henry Clay and his good friend Stephen Girard. Hunting was often part of the routine for guests. One day Joseph reported that while he was hunting in his woods at Pointe Breeze he saw — the Jersey Devil!

I don't think the creature was invited.

Part Six:
Afterthoughts

My dear companion of fifteen years passed over in 1996. I'll refer to him as Ange. It took a few years for me to settle down internally, but when I did I noticed a few things happening. I just recorded them. I'll leave it up to you to think what you may.

January 13, 2000:

Living alone I tend to have little routines that I do automatically without thinking. Before I headed upstairs to go to sleep, I put the house to sleep. I locked the kitchen door, turned off the lights, picked up my keys and glanced around to see that everything was straightened up and neat. I see no sense in coming downstairs in the morning to a mess. I may as well start the day looking at a neat house.

Of course the really last thing before I turned out the light was to check the thermostat, to be sure it wasn't turned up too high, but high enough that the tenants in my apartment building weren't cold. That done I was ready for bed.

The next morning I came downstairs and, as soon as my foot left the last step, I saw it. The dining room ceiling fan was on. The ceiling fan Ange insisted on installing when I didn't want it. The same ceiling fan that had not been used since the summer before. This was January and it was cold outside! In order to turn the fan on, I had to reach over the table and pull the chain. It was impossible for it to go on accidentally. I wondered was this a little message from him letting me know he's okay?

December 13, 2000:

In the corner of my kitchen over top of my sink cabinet hung a tiffany-style lamp that was given to me as a gift after Ange passed over. It had a switch on the lamp, but it was so high that instead of climbing up on a chair to turn it on and off each day, I pulled the plug from the outlet.

When I went to plug the cord into the outlet. I found the lamp was turned off at the light switch!

January 13, 2002:

On Sunday morning after cleaning the kitchen I closed and locked the kitchen door but left the kitchen radio on.

It was my habit to have all the radios in the house set to a Philadelphia FM station that played all and only Elvis Presley music on Sunday mornings. It was a unique program because it offered Elvis' practice sessions, unreleased versions of his music, and sometimes his conversations. The program provided a pleasant, thoughtful trip back to my teen years.

So, with all the radios on and tuned to the same station, I moved through the house while his music flowed from room to room with me. I purposely left the living room radio on, too. I turned it up loud so it complimented my upstairs radio. Next I went upstairs to shower and dress for an afternoon lecture. When I came downstairs an hour later, the radios were turned off. Ange never tolerated Elvis Presley music in the house. When he was still alive we played Italian music only. This was the same date, but two years after the first incident.

July 1, 2005:

After I sold my business, I moved my office into my guest bedroom. I still had a lot of inventory that didn't go with the sale and it was all piled in the hallway. One day I was busy loading some items onto an Internet auction. After so many hours at the computer I thought it was time for a little break and a good stretch.

So I made room on the bed, moving items aside. I had been taking pictures of them to sell. I layed down and leisurely looked at the bookcase that is built within what was once a doorway. The doorway had been closed off before I bought the building.

The book on the top shelf, a hundred plus years old, stood atilt. It lost its hardcover boards long ago. As I lay gazing at it, the first page opened, fluttered, and laid back against the bulk again. That's all. No more. No breeze in here. No wind of any kind. No other book affected.

Curious, I got up and stretched across the inventory piled in boxes at the base of the bookcase. I found it was an Italian Primer, written in Italian. 'Ange is still with me.' I thought. I just knew he was right there with me, giving me a message. I took the book and gave it to his daughter. I felt it belonged with her.

July 2005:

Soon after I delivered the book, I entered my guest room/office and, to my complete surprise, the copy machine started up and printed out a blank sheet!

Bibliography

Berube, Claude and Rodgaard, John. *A Call to the Sea*. Dulles, Virginia: Potomac Books, 2005.

Blum, Deborah. *Ghost Hunters, William James and the Search for Scientific Proof of Life After Death*. Dulles, Virginia: Penguin Press, 2006.

Blum, Deborah. "Ghosts in the Medicine." New York, New York: *New York Times*, 2007.

Bordentown Area Bicentennial Committee and the Bordentown Historical Society. *Bordentown: 1682-1976*. Bordentown, New Jersey: Bordentown Historical Society, 1977.

Burr, E. Samuel Jr. *Small Town Merchant*. New York, New York: Vantage Press, 1957.

Davis, W. William H., A. M. *History of Bucks County, Pennsylvania*. New York-Chicago: Lewis Publishing Co., 1905.

Davis, W. W. H. *Early Settlers of Bucks County, Pennsylvania*. Doylestown Meeting, Pennsylvania: 1895.

Fackenthal, Jr., B. F. *Improving Navigation on the Delaware River*. Allentown, Pennsylvania: Bucks County Historical Society, 1932.

Woodward, E. M. *History of Burlington County*. "Biographical Sketch of Colonel Joseph Kirkbride." Burlington, New Jersey: Burlington County Historical Society.

Index

Aaronson, Marion, 123
Adams, John Quincy, 153
Adrienne, 116
Africa, 121
Allentown, New Jersey, 128
American Navy, 118, 119
American Red Cross, 108
Amsterdam, Netherlands, 96
Angel of the Battlefield, 108
Antietam Battle, 31
Arch Street Quaker Meeting House, 31
Asbury Park, New Jersey, 96
Atlantic Ocean, 81

Barge Creek, 131
Barry, Captain John, 81
Barton, Clara, 107, 108, 109, 110, 111, 112, 113, 114
Bellevue, 127, 128, 129, 131, 132
Black Rangers of Suriname, 121
Black's Creek, 60, 94
Block, Mr., 122
Board of Education, 109
Bonaparte, Joseph, 40, 120, 152
Bonaparte, Napoleon, 152
Boni-Maroon War, 121, 154
Boni-Maroons, 121
Borden Family, 115
Borden, Captain Joseph, 128
Borden, Colonel Joseph, 125
Bordentown Banking Company, 97
Bordentown City, 60, 70, 71, 75, 82, 92, 98, 105, 122, 134, 145, 150
Bordentown Estate, 129
Bordentown Historical Society, 108, 111, 115, 158
Bordentown Memorial Fund, 104

Bordentown Military Institute, 82, 96
Bordentown Yacht Club, 87
Bossert Estates, 135, 141
Bossert, Charles, 141
Boston, Massachusetts, 119
British, 11, 81, 118, 125, 128
Brooklyn, New York, 53
Bunting Brothers, 125
Burr, Anna Thompson, 133, 134
Burr, Elizabeth Thompson, 133
Burr, Samuel Engle, Jr., 133
Burr's Corner, 133
Buster Brown, 112

California, 74
Camden & Amboy Railroad, 87, 97, 122
Camden, New Jersey, 104
Canada, 115
Cape Horn, South America, 129
Carman, Caleb, 125
Carter, David, 129
Chamber of Commerce, 123
Chapel Lane (now West Church Street), 129
Charleston, South Carolina, 81
Chestnut Street, 56
Christmas, 39, 46, 95, 107, 110, 128, 129, 130
Cimarron, 81
Citizens' Hook & Ladder Firehouse, 88
Civil War, 31, 81, 108, 115, 133
Claverack near Hudson, New York, 96
Clay, Henry, 153
Colt, Dr. Henry, 32
Common Sense, 127

Cranbury, New Jersey, 143, 144
Crosswicks Creek, 81, 94, 135
Crosswicks Street, 133
Cyane, 118

Daniels, Elizabeth Urbanski, 12, 59, 63
Davis, Varina Howell (Mrs. Jefferson), 133
Decatur, Stephan, 119
Decatur, Stephen, 152
Delaware River, 17, 52, 71, 81, 82, 86, 94, 115, 118 -121, 125, 127, 128, 150, 158
Divine Word Seminary, 52
Dunker Church, 31
Dutch West Indies, 96

East Burlington Street, 107
East Union Street, 97
Elizabeth Street, 71
Emperor Napoleon III, 120

Farnsworth Avenue, 34, 49, 65, 71, 91, 92, 96, 105, 107, 115, 123, 133
Farnsworth's Landing, 81, 115
Firehouse Art Gallery, 104
Florida, 55, 64, 77
Footprints, 70, 131
Frederici, Francois, 119, 121
Frederici, Juriaan Francois, 121

General of Suriname, 119
Ghost Walk, 12, 115, 116, 124, 127, 133
Gilmore, Fred, 122
Girard, Stephen, 153
Gunner, 42

Harvey Cedars, New Jersey, 123
Havilland, Richard, 129
Herron, Dr. John, 74
Hessians, 87, 128
Hightstown, New Jersey, 107, 146
Hoagland, Colonel Oakey, 125
Holiday Rout, 111, 112
Holy Assumption Cemetery, Burlington County, New Jersey, 87

India, 129
Ireland, 104, 120
Irish Home Rule, 120
Italian Primer, 157

Jackaway, Robert, 125
Jefferson, President Thomas, 120
Jersey Devil, 152, 153

Kachina Doll, 55
Kirkbride Ferry Service, 127
Kirkbride, Colonel Joseph and wife Phoebe, 127
Kirkbride, Joseph, 127
Kirkbride, Mary, 128

Lafayette, Marquis de, 153
Lamson, Joshua, 81
Leeds, Mrs., 152
Lenni Lenape, 54,135,150
Levant, 118
Lincoln, President Abraham, 51, 120
Local Defense Council, 105
Lundeen, Aunt May, 123

Madeira, Portugal, 118
Madison, President James, 120
Madrid, 119
Main Street, 91, 125
Mansfield Township, New Jersey, 71
Massage room, 26
Mauch Chunk (now Jim Thorpe), Pennsylvania, 104
McCall, Captain Edward R., 81
Mershon, D. S., 81
Mill Street, 89
Miller's Field, 31
Mingo, 82
Monmouth Junction, New Jersey, 104
Montpellier, 119
Moorestown, New Jersey, 133
Mount Holly, New Jersey, 104
Munsi, 150

Native Americans, 54, 135, 150
Naval Academy, 82
New York Harbor, New York, 125

Old Ironsides, 118-121
Old Opera House, 147
Old Stone Shanty, 121, 122

Pacific Ocean, 82
Pacific Submarine Telegraph, 82, 119
Paine, Thomas, 127, 128
Paleo-Native Americans, 150
Paramaribo, Suriname, South American Dutch Colony, 121
Paris, France, 129, 131
Park Street, 50, 52, 136
Parnell Charles Stewart, 120
Parnell, Delia Stewart, 120
Parnell, Fanny, 120
Penn's Manor, 127
Pennsbury Manor, Bucks County, Pennsylvania, 127
Pennsylvania, 104, 115, 127, 158
Pennsylvania Railroad, 97, 104
Perth Amboy, New Jersey, 46
Philadelphia Harbor, 125, 128
Philadelphia Naval Yard, 119
Philadelphia, Pennsylvania, 32
Pine Barrens, New Jersey, 152
Plowman, Joseph, 125
Point Pleasant, New Jersey, 104
Pointe Breeze, 152, 153
Pow Wow, 55
Presley, Elvis, 156
Princeton, 75, 115

Quaker, 34, 54, 55, 107, 115, 135
Quaker Burying Ground, 30

Realtor, 40, 60, 143, 144, 145
Renssalaerwyck, Patroon, 96
Revolutionary War, 32, 81, 87, 125, 128
Riggi, Anna May Bice, 12, 59
Rights of Man, 127
Rockwell, Aunt Ople, 123
Rogers, Mary, 128
Rogers, Samuel, 128
Rush, Richard, 119
Russo-Japanese War, 82

Saylor, Stella, 97
Schoolhouse, 107 - 114
Sea Girt, New Jersey, 104

Secord, Captain, 128, 129
Secord, Helen, 129-131
Sharpsburg, Maryland, 31
Shoppe 202 Antiques, 96
Smith, Charlotte, 120
Smith, Edward, 120
Smith, Julia, 120
Smith, Margaret, 120
South Amboy, New Jersey, 104
Spanish-American War, 82
St. Mary's School, 71
Stacy, Mahlon and Rebeckah, 127
Station B East, 115
Stewart, Charles, 81, 118, 120, 122
Stewart, Commodore Charles, 81
Stewart, Delia, 120
Stewart, Marion, 123
Straus, Nathan, 32
Sweden, 104
Swift Mansion, 94, 96
Swift, George W., Jr. and wife Stella (Saylor), 97

Tarot cards, 63, 84
Toots'n Reds Bar, 105
Trenton, New Jersey, 53, 104, 115, 127, 139
Tudor, Delia, 119

Unami, 135, 150
Underground Railroad, 115, 116
Upstate New York, 40
USS Constitution, 118
USS Franklin, 119

Van Renssalaer, Robert Schuyler and wife Virginia, 97
Venezuela, 38, 39
Victorian, 26, 91, 94, 143, 145

Walnut Street, 88, 104, 126
Waretown, New Jersey Mennonites, 149
Washington, George, Martha, 96
Washington, President George, 120
Webster, Daniel, 153
West Street, 65, 107
White Hill, Burlington County, New Jersey, 122
William MacFarland High School, 139
World War I, 104
World War II, 105